EKKLESIA

THE GOVERNMENT

OF THE KINGDOM OF

HEAVEN ON EARTH

JOE NICOLA

Spring Mill Publishing

Sharpsburg, Maryland USA

First Printing: 2014

ISBN: 978-1500454685

Cover design by James Nesbit.

Editing, text design and typesetting by Jim Bryson.

Copy editing by Karen Crawley.

Acknowledgments

The Ekklesia is rising across the globe, and Joe Nicola's new book is at the forefront of that movement. Highly readable and comprehensive, the core ideas behind this work of God are made easily accessible to anyone with a hunger to know where the church is headed next. I have worked with Joe Nicola and have come to regard him as a man of integrity and one simple passion: to see the church grow into the role that Jesus destined for it. Joe's heart for God's people is on display through these pages as he echoes the heart of the Father.

Apostle Clay Nash

Author of *Activating The Prophetic.*

****

I have worked with Joe and Renee Nicola for several years now in our global ministries network. Joe, is a man of God, with a heart to see transformation in the body of Christ. This book takes us on his journey into an understanding of our true spiritual authority as the ekklesia of God in the earth. I highly recommend this transcript to those who are hungering to know more about their true spiritual authority before the throne, and I commend Joe Nicola for his ability to communicate these concepts in an easily understood, Biblically-based transcript.

Regina Shank, Apostolic Leader

Missouri Prayer Global Ministries

Network Ekklesia International

****

Our culture is longing for restoration in these last days. Joe's message challenges the status quo and shows that needed changes are coming (Acts 3:21). Joe reveals how the Ekklesia is being restored, the same Ekklesia that Jesus said He would build. The Ekklesia is glorious and has all authority through Christ Jesus on the earth. You will understand just what the Lord had in mind and how His church is to function. With immediate relevance and urgency, Joe's work is a must-read for every believer!

Kamal Saleem

Author of *The Blood of Lambs* and the *Unveiling Series.*

Table of Contents

Dedication

I dedicate this book to my Lord, my Savior, and the Lover of my soul, Jesus, who found me when I was so lost I couldn't find myself. He came to me and loved me and was affectionate to me even though I didn't deserve it.

I also dedicate this book to my wife Renee who loves me unconditionally and is my best friend. You have continued to believe in me and spur me on to be all I can be. I love you with all that is in me, and I am grateful to the Lord for bringing us together.

I want to thank my congregation who have encouraged me, prayed for me and supported me. It is so fun to live life with you!

Introduction

What comes to mind when you hear the word "church?" The Bible tells us in Matthew 16:18 that Jesus said He would build His church. What would the disciples have thought Jesus meant since they had not heard the word "church" before? When Matthew wrote his gospel, he used the Greek language. The word he chose that is translated as "church" in English is ekklesia. Ekklesia was a common word during the time that Jesus walked the earth.

Over time, we have lost the true meaning of this word and how it applies to us today. In Genesis 1:28, God commissioned man at creation with fruitfulness, multiplication, and the task of subduing and ruling the Earth. In Matthew 28:18-20, Jesus gave us a commission that restates God's original assignment to disciple the nations.

I wrote this book to help people understand the true meaning of what Jesus said He would build. We will discuss the history, usage and application of this word for today. This book, however, is just the beginning. It will help us rediscover Jesus' original intent when He said, "upon this rock I will build My church, and the gates of Hades will not overpower it."

...upon this rock I will build My church; and the gates of Hades will not overpower it.

Matthew 16:18

He will reign over the house of Jacob forever, and His kingdom will have no end.

Luke 1:3

There will be no end to the increase of His government or of peace, on the throne of David and over his kingdom, to establish it and to uphold it with justice and righteousness from then on and forevermore. The zeal of the LORD of hosts will accomplish this.

Isaiah 9:7

Chapter 1

My Personal Journey

When I was born again at 20, I dreamed of owning my own business—a motorcycle repair shop. After being a mechanic for a few years and being passionate about doing what I loved, the Lord spoke to me to launch out and start my own business. Thankfully, for eight years, God made that possible. I was a motorcycle mechanic and business owner, and I took great pride in that. I learned a lot during that time. What I was unaware of was that God was training me for another type of ministry. Working on motorcycles and owning my own business, it turned out, was only temporary.

At 27, I accepted a part-time youth pastor position while still running my business. Then at 31, the Lord began a change in me, and I knew I had to answer a call to shut my business down and go into full-time youth ministry. However, I fought God on this. Up until this point in my life, the toughest thing God had asked me to do was to be a youth pastor. The second hardest thing was to shut my business down and stop working on motorcycles. But thankfully, God won. I sold my tools and equipment and closed my business in July of 1994, feeling like my heart had been ripped from my chest. I felt lost. The only way I knew to make a living and do what I loved was gone.

I knew there wasn't much money in being a youth pastor. So I tried to continue being a part-time youth pastor while selling life and health insurance to supplement my income. I went to school, passed my tests and received my certification. But I was a fish out of water. I hated it. This was not what God called me to do.

I thought everything had changed for the better when my pastor called one day and asked me to stop by his office. We talked for a bit, and then he offered me a full-time position as youth pastor. I thought Praise God! I don't have to keep trying to sell insurance! Then he slid a piece a paper across his desk towards me. It was an employee contract with my salary on it. I looked at it, and my heart sank. I couldn't believe it--$13,200 a year? I hadn't made so little money since high school. He had to be kidding; I couldn't live on that. I felt my financial goals swirl down the drain. $13,200 a year! That can't be God!

Then I heard God speak: *Take it.* So I took it.

When I went home to tell my wife, I leaned against our refrigerator and cried. I told her I would not be able to provide for her as I planned. She worked full-time selling real estate at the time. I remember her giving me that look that only wives can give as she countered my logic: *What difference does it make whether God uses me or you to provide the finances needed?* Well, to a man, it makes a huge difference! But, I knew she was right. (Two people I should never argue with: God and my wife—not necessarily in that order.)

In obedience to my calling, I spent the next five years as a full-time youth pastor. And just as I did when I sold my business, I learned a lot working in ministry.

As a congregation member, I'd always wondered about the lack of authentic life in our gatherings—the difference between what I saw in the Word of God and what I saw in many church services, conferences, meetings and the everyday lives of Christians—even my own life.

I saw many good people working jobs, striving to serve God, providing for their families and generally doing what they thought was expected of them, but they seemed a little disconnected and powerless. Yet I always attributed that lack to the fundamental weakness of the parishioners—converts covered by Jesus' blood, culled from a spiritually dull and apathetic society. It must be our lack of faith and obedience, I thought. In turn, I sympathized with pastors and others in Christian leadership who struggled to do their best with those who came wandering through the door.

All that changed when I began to observe life from the other side of the altar. Stepping into ministry—first as a youth pastor and later as a head pastor—revealed the inner workings of the church; a view beyond the curtain. Sadly, what I saw was underwhelming. I discovered a lack of power, direction, and apathy among some of the leadership. In trying to understand the source, however, I found that the congregation blamed their leaders and the leaders blamed their congregations. Neither side took full responsibility, and neither side seemed satisfied.

I found many leaders who had given up and were just trying to maintain. A few still earnestly sought God, but others were recoiling from once having reached out to the sea of humanity with idealistic fervor, only to be tossed back to shore with a revised mindset deemed more practical and reality-based. Many —too many—were stressed out, over-burdened, weighed down and over worked. The majority, but certainly not all, had succumbed to a business mentality rather than embracing a kingdom mindset. They operated their local churches with a focus on increasing attendance, monetary flow and programs, while neglecting the supernatural power of the Holy Spirit. Tragically, I also found committed leaders drowning in a sea of impossible expectations and entrenched apathy. Many good people across the country had simply given up and quit the ministry.

When the Lord spoke to me about starting a church, I told Him that if this was what being a pastor was all about, I did not want it. He replied: *I didn't ask you to.* That was all He needed to say; I knew there was a better way. My heart yearned to see the church free, alive, and productive. As I sought God on behalf of the people who were being broken by the very organization that should have been helping them, I realized that this could not be what Jesus died for. We needed to change. We had to move forward. We had to move out of this manmade, business mindset and into what began in the Book of Acts. We had to advance to become what Jesus called us to be.

In my search, I began to question everything.

Is this what church is all about?

Is this what God intended His children to be and to accomplish?

Why are we so weak and powerless?

How has the church become a business?

With all the outreaches, events and even the sheer number of churches in America, why does our culture look more like Hell than Heaven?

The Bible tells us that Jesus is returning for a beautiful, victorious bride, not one hiding in defeat, battered and bruised. When I read the promises and provisions the Lord has given to us now in this life, I realize that so many of us live like beggars. Most of us are just existing, waiting for Jesus to return and straighten the whole mess out.

Is this the abundant life Jesus came to give us? Have we missed something? I knew the problem was with us and not the Lord.

Jesus said He was going to build something glorious, against which the gates of Hell would not prevail. Do we have what He intended or is there something else that we have missed all along? God created us to subdue the Earth and rule over it. If this is true, why are we letting the world rule us? He made us priests and kings! We were created to rule and reign with Him now and for all eternity!

There had to be more!

Over several years, as I pursued the answers, the Lord began revealing that the answers had to do with what Jesus actually said He would build (in Matthew 16), and I slowly began to realize that these truths had been misunderstood for centuries. As I began to understand what Jesus really intended, everything changed!

I realized that the fault was not with the lost and wandering congregation, nor was it with the leadership struggling to maintain the status quo. Instead, it was an overall lack of understanding of who and what Jesus called His church to be.

When Christians comprehend who they truly are, congregations will stand ready to serve and follow, and leadership will stand ready to serve and lead. And most remarkably, the Holy Spirit will flow to restore the Kingdom of God to the Earth, starting with us—the Bride of Christ—and permeate every facet of society, bringing a kingdom culture to construction jobsites, office buildings, local cafes, multinational corporations, and yes, even to motorcycle shops across this great land.

So what did Jesus actually say He would build? What is it? How does it function? Most importantly: how do we get there from here? We need to compare the traditional church—as man has built it—to what Jesus said He would build.

The heart of God is to reach every man and woman. He sent Jesus to establish His kingdom so that His spirit could flow through it and touch every heart, save every soul.

Let us begin our journey with an understanding of God's plan and purpose for each one of us as revealed through scripture.

Chapter 2

Sons of God

Despite the woeful condition of the modern church, we actually live in exciting times. The Lord is restoring principles to His people that have been lost for generations; truths that we need to embrace if we are to become who we are called to be. In the busyness and turmoil of these modern times, we easily let go of the greater truths of our identity and calling for the immediacy of the moment. But God, in His mercy, has not turned his back on us. As wave after of wave of revelation pours out upon the Earth in response to our heart-cries, we must awaken and realize our position of authority over the Earth as sons and daughters of the Living God, called to be the Body of Jesus Christ.

In order for the church to rise up in victory and power, we must strengthen each individual component of Christ's Body, that means each one of us. Without revelation of who we are as individuals in Christ, we can't really function to our full potential in our place and calling in the Body—whether we are a foot, hand, eye, ear, or any other body part. And while we can be born again without being a part of a local congregation, the converse is not true. We cannot be effective members of a local congregation without understanding our God-given identity.

As we delve into Jesus' intentions for His church, we need to appreciate the building blocks He is using to build it: the sons of God.

Also, please note that I use the term "son" the way many texts use "man," for mankind, in a purely genderless connotation. "Son" simply means offspring—male and female alike.

> *God created man in His own image, in the image of God He created him; male and female He created them.*
>
> Genesis 1:27

If we are going to subdue the Earth and rule over it, accomplishing all that Jesus commissioned us to do, it is crucial that we know who we are as sons of God.

So who are the sons of God?

Who Are You Now?

As I said in chapter 1, prior to entering full-time ministry, I owned a motorcycle parts and repair shop. At that time, if you had asked me who I was, I would have said a motorcycle mechanic and business owner. I received most of my significance from these titles and activities. Unfortunately, my identity was based on what I did and owned, not on who I truly was. As long as I performed well, pleased others, and made money, my self-worth was inflated. But if the opposite happened, I could easily become deflated and feel devalued. It was an up and down existence that God would soon rescue me from.

If we belong to God, He will eventually force the question of identity upon us, often kicking away the supports that give superficial meaning and value to our lives. But He will also compel us to dig deep in the Word to discover what He really sees in us. Further, His Spirit will reveal what we truly think of ourselves; our true self-image when the people are gone, the distractions removed, and the false props exposed for what they really are.

For me, this point came when the Lord called me to stop repairing motorcycles, sell my business, and work full time in a congregation as a youth pastor. This was not an easy call to answer. Like I said before, my heart felt like it was being ripped from me, but I knew I had to obey God. All I had ever known in life was motorcycles, and I loved it. I didn't know how to make a living any other way. My security was gone. I felt empty and lost. Little did I know at the time that before God fills us, He empties us.

I sold all of my equipment and most of my hand tools so that it would be impossible to work on motorcycles even if I wanted to. I recalled the Vikings who, upon arriving on the shores of a land they were invading, would first torch the boats that brought them there, ensuring that there was no means of easy retreat. My boats were burning, the bitter smoke rising to heaven, and my journey just beginning. At that low point of my life, God asked me a question that changed me forever:

Who are you now?

Of course, I didn't know the answer—that is why He asked me! And so I began a quest to answer the question that God had planted deep in my unexplored heart.

In the process, I discovered that most of us face the same dilemma. We define our identity from our occupation, our performance, even our ministry title instead of God's definition of us. While each of these are important, we have to wonder what happens to us when these things no longer exist—when we can no longer turn a wrench, when performance standards become unreachable, or when our ministry shifts or dissolves altogether.

It is imperative that each of us discover the answer to who we are and find the value God has placed within us as His children without reference to our career, job, position, title, marriage or parenthood. The bottom line is this: apart from all that we do or cherish, we must learn that we are valuable simply because God values us.

All human beings have great value and worth because of who God created us to be. We are created with the ability to have an intimate relationship with our Heavenly Father and to be a temple of the Holy Spirit living within us. We are so valued in His sight that He placed the same value on us as He did His first-born Son Jesus. No matter what you have to sell, it is only worth what someone is willing to pay for it. The buyer determines the value. God the Father determined our worth or value by the price He paid for our redemption—the life of Christ Jesus!

The Redeemed

The Bible makes it clear that all humans are His creation, but not all are His children. When Adam and Eve sinned, they handed over their delegated authority to Satan, and a curse was released into the world that brought death.

Sin is a perversion of God's created order and has a corrupting effect on everything it touches. God said that if the first man ate from the Tree of the Knowledge of Good and Evil he would surely die. Death was the consequence that affected each part of man's being: body, soul and spirit. Today, we live with the effects of that sin; our bodies age and we grow old. Further, our bodies are susceptible to sickness and disease and eventually die. Aside from eventual death, our souls (our mind, will and emotions) are stained and altered. We see an example of this when Adam and Eve's eyes were opened and they were afraid, hiding themselves from God and excusing their transgression. When challenged, Adam blamed God and Eve (*"The woman whom You gave to be with me..."*) for eating the fruit, while Eve blamed the serpent (*"The serpent deceived me"*). Not sure who the serpent blamed.

Our spirit was also affected which corrupted our nature. All men inherit a corrupted nature from Adam. When Adam sinned, death—the corruption of life—was the result, and caused a separation between man and God. The union that Adam and God enjoyed was severed because of sin. This is the death that God told Adam would happen if he ate from the Tree.

The good news is that 2 Corinthians 5:16 says we become new creatures when we receive Jesus by being born again. In the born-again experience, we receive a new spirit created in the image of God. It is at this exact moment we become a child of God.

> *But as many as received Him, to them He gave the right to become children of God, even to those who believe in His name, who were born, not of blood nor of the will of the flesh nor of the will of man, but of God.*
>
> John 1:12-13

Notice this passage says that whoever "receives" Jesus and is born of God is given the right to become a child of God. Of course, we cannot *become* something we already are. If all humans are already children of God, then how is it possible or even necessary to *become* a child of God? The truth is that we only become the children of God when we receive Jesus.

Becoming a child of God is not just a figurative act; it is an actual conversion. As newly birthed offspring, we literally have the seed of God planted in us.

> No one who is born of God practices sin, because His seed abides in him; and he cannot sin, because he is born of God.

> 1 John 3:9

The word for "seed" here is the Greek word *sperma,* which is the English word "sperm." It is important that we know what is in sperm. Biologically, the most important element in sperm for our discussion is DNA—deoxyribonucleic acid—which is the hereditary material that lies within the nucleus of all cells in humans and other living organisms.

Spiritually, we actually become a child of God, sharing the DNA of God when we are born again. All that is in God is now in those who are children of God. This is similar to when God breathed into Adam, and he became a living being (Genesis 2:7). God's breath represents His Spirit. The life and nature of God was breathed into Adam, just as in the born-again experience today. God breathes into us and causes us to be born again with new life. We actually become a new creation with new life.

> Therefore if anyone is in Christ, he is a new creature; the old things passed away; behold, new things have come.

> 2 Corinthians 5:16

Knowing that we are *new creatures* and that *old things passed away,* is vital for accomplishing all that the Lord has for us to do. I believe that most Christians do not know their true identity as sons and daughters of God. Statements like, *"I am a sinner saved by grace"* and *"we are all sinners"* fail to express how our nature changes when we are born again. Nowhere in the New Testament is a reborn child of God called a sinner unless they have strayed from the truth and are living a lifestyle of unrepentant sin (James 5:19-20). Yes, all are sinners until they receive Christ and are born again (Romans 5:8). It is also true that we are saved by grace (Ephesians 2:8-9). However, when we are born again, we are no longer defined by sin even though we may still sin. Sin is no longer part of our nature or identity. To say anything less about ourselves than what God says is ignorance or pride. Paul makes it very clear in Romans:

> *For through the grace given to me I say to everyone among you not to think more highly of himself than he ought to think; but to think so as to have sound judgment, as God has allotted to each a measure of faith.*

> Romans 12:3

Please notice the subtle word play in this scripture which has profound implications. The Bible says to "not think more highly of ourselves than we ought." It doesn't say to avoid thinking highly of ourselves.

You see, what was natural before Adam and Eve sinned is now unnatural. We use the term supernatural to mean things that are not natural or normal occurrences. We talk about living a supernatural life which is a life led by the Spirit of God where healing, miracles, signs and wonders happen on a regular basis. This is normal Kingdom living. To God, the supernatural is natural. To Adam and Eve before the Fall, the supernatural was natural. The curse, which is a result of sin and the fall of mankind in the Garden, reduced man's life to a natural existence. When Jesus came to Earth, He lived a supernatural life and paved the way for us to do the same. Walking on water is not natural. Healing the blind is not natural. Multiplying bread and fish is not natural. Pulling money from the mouth of a fish is not natural. Loving the unlovely is not natural. God's natural is supernatural. Life in the Kingdom of God is naturally supernatural. This is the abundant life that Jesus came to give us, as John tells us:

> I came that they may have life, and have it abundantly.
>
> John 10:10

Adoption

Jesus did more than provide forgiveness for sin. As *the firstborn among many brethren* (Romans 8:29), He enabled a new birth for all who receive Him. In this rebirth something remarkable happens: Jesus not only becomes our Lord and our Savior, but also our elder brother. Through God's DNA, we are transferred into the same bloodline as Jesus, with the same potential to be Christ-like and live the supernatural life that He lived.

> Truly, truly, I say to you, he who believes in Me, the works that I do, he will do also; and greater works than these he will do; because I go to the Father.
>
> John 14:12

Not only does God the Father cause us to be born again, but He also adopts each of us as His new sons and daughters, giving us full, legal inheritance rights! (Galatians 4:5, Romans 8:15 and Ephesians 1:5). This adoption process is not the same as we are familiar with today where someone finds a non-biological child then goes through a legal process to make him their own. The adoption process the Bible is speaking about is based on Roman law where the father had to actually choose whether or not to adopt his own biological son. Only when the father made the choice and adopted him did the son become his legal heir. If the Roman father did not adopt his son, that son would not have a legal right to an inheritance.

Unlike the Roman custom, we have been unconditionally adopted by God. We are true heirs with Jesus. God has predestined us to adoption as sons, meaning that everyone who receives Jesus and is born again has been guaranteed adoption by God and given full legal inheritance rights!

A New Kingdom

Before we were born again, we lived under the "domain of darkness," which is ruled by Satan (Colossians 1:13). The domain of darkness operates by "the law of sin and death" (Romans 8:2). Our minds were in darkness, leading us to sin and eventually, death. In other words, we were clueless about God and His kingdom. But when we came out of darkness and into the Kingdom of light, the Holy Spirit began illuminating us. So, we must cooperate by changing the way we think and begin receiving revelation about our new identity in Christ as sons of God in order to start living according to the Kingdom of Heaven. Therefore, it is absolutely necessary that we renew our minds with the Word of God (Romans 12:2).

We not only must renew our minds, but we must also understand that we have been given the grace or power to live by the Spirit, which means that as we yield our lives to the Holy Spirit, we have grace to not only overcome sin but also to rule and reign with Christ Jesus over the Earth.

In the next chapter, we will begin to look at what Jesus said He would build and how that ties in with our identity as sons of God. Understanding our new identity as sons and daughters of God will be vital for the remainder of this book.

Jesus intends to build His church with quality materials. That would be us: redeemed of God, adopted sons, full heirs with Christ, living in a new kingdom. As children of God, we carry the authority of Father.

Let's see how this plays out as we endeavor to understand Jesus' true intentions for His church.

Chapter 3

Authority

The heavens are the heavens of the Lord, but the Earth He has given to the sons of men.

Psalm 115:16

Authority is good; it gets things done. Authority is the power and the right to act. However, just like Adam and Eve, our authority is supported by God only as long as we are born again and in submission to Him. The Jewish exorcists in Acts found this out the hard way.

> *But also some of the Jewish exorcists, who went from place to place, attempted to name over those who had the evil spirits the name of the Lord Jesus, saying, "I adjure you by Jesus whom Paul preaches." Seven sons of one Sceva, a Jewish chief priest, were doing this. And the evil spirit answered and said to them, "I recognize Jesus, and I know about Paul, but who are you?"*

Acts 19:13-15

The evil spirit only recognized those who belonged to the Lord, those whose authority came from being in submission to Him. *"I recognize Jesus and know about Paul, but who are you?"* The seven sons of Sceva were using the name of Jesus without being true sons of God and therefore without true authority.

This lesson is as true today as it was in Paul's time. The name of Jesus is not a talisman. Evil spirits only obey true authority. When we are born again, we submit to God and He begins to delegate His authority to us. When we exercise our authority in Christ, demons obey!

Powerful!

You see, God has ultimate authority over everything, and, all authority flows from Him. But at creation, He delegated some of His authority over the Earth to man.

> *God blessed them; and God said to them, "Be fruitful and multiply, and fill the Earth, and subdue it; and rule over the fish of the sea and over the birds of the sky and over every living thing that moves on the Earth."*
>
> Genesis 1:28

Please note the conditional nature of man's position. As long as he remained submitted to God, he retained the authority to fulfill God's commission to subdue the Earth, bringing it under man's rule and God's rule. What a great deal.

Incidentally, God intended for man to reign over the Earth; man—not Satan, or demons, or animals, or any other created being. In Genesis when Adam exercised his right to name the animals, he did so through the authority God gave him, meaning that man was in authority over these creatures from the beginning. Unfortunately, man did not retain his authority for long. It is also interesting to note that God did not give man authority to subdue and rule over other men in order to control and manipulate them.

Paradise Lost

When man sinned in the Garden he surrendered his delegated authority to the one that he obeyed: Satan.

> *you are slaves of the one whom you obey, either of sin resulting in death, or of obedience resulting in righteousness?*
>
> Romans 6:16

Evidence of man's lost authority can be seen throughout scripture. Let's look at Jesus' temptation by Satan in the wilderness.

> *And he [Satan] led Him up and showed Him all the kingdoms of the world in a moment of time. And the devil said to Him, "I will give You all this domain and its glory; for it has been handed over to me, and I give it to whomever I wish."*
>
> Luke 4:5-6

Who handed Satan *"this domain and glory?"* Well...*man*, that's who. Satan has limited authority over the Earth—the authority that was handed to him by Adam. Still, God retained ultimate authority and control. Even though the first man and woman sinned, losing their authority and the place from which they were to rule—the Garden of Eden—God never changed His mind about man subduing and ruling the Earth.

For the gifts and the calling of God are irrevocable.

Romans 11:29

That means that our authority is still ours, if we want it. But we have to accept it, we have to take it, and we have to hold on to it, growing in our ability to exercise it.

Of course, if taking authority seems too much work, think of the converse. If we, as redeemed sons of God, do not take authority over our lives, our communities, our local churches, and our world... who will? Certainly, one may respond: *Well, God! That's who.* But if we are reluctant to take up the very authority He has given us, what makes us think that God will step in and supplement that authority gap?

Show me the parent who taught their child to do the dishes by cleaning every cup, plate, spoon and pot that the child ever dirtied and tossed aside. Yes, children learn from example, but the example set is often not what we think. The child will learn that Mom or Dad cleans the dishes, period! And Christians will learn that God does everything, so they need do nothing. That is, assuming God would be willing to set such an example. Fortunately, God is smarter than we are.

So it comes down to this simple proposition: we, who have been called to assume our position in God's Kingdom, relinquish our God-given authority as the Redeemed of Christ and lead others to do the same, who will take that authority? Obviously, the one who wanted it bad enough to steal it in the first place. And for what end? Our benefit or his?

We have a choice: to walk in the authority we have been given—ruling, reigning and being restored with Christ in this life, or to be ruled by the domain of darkness and inherit the wind. Each of us has an Eden to hold or lose; we can struggle with thorns by the sweat of our brow, or walk with God in the nearness of spirit. Our choice could not be clearer.

Replenish the Earth

Most people understand that God created man with the ability to bear offspring and multiply, thereby fulfilling the commission to be fruitful and replenish the Earth. But do we realize that this should be applied in the spiritual as well as the natural?

In the natural, we bear children and populate the Earth (which man obviously has no trouble doing). In the spiritual, however, we lead others to Christ, bearing spiritual offspring and thereby replenishing a fallen Earth with the redeemed of the Lord.

Repopulating is the easy part; even making disciples of Christ is progressing across the globe, albeit with some strong religious overtones at times. But do we understand why God wants us to (spiritually) repopulate the Earth? Is it just that He likes people? Or disciples? Well, yes and no. In truth, there is more to the plan than one big happy Earth-family.

As we saw a few paragraphs before, God created us to subdue the Earth and rule over it. These words were in God's original commission to man. The word "subdue" means to bring under control by force, to conquer, bring into bondage or subjection. That's pretty strong. And the word "rule" means to have dominion, to dominate. God created man to rule the Earth with Him.

Yes, we are having babies—natural and spiritual—but are we fulfilling our whole commission? Are we subduing the Earth? As we look at the world today, can we honestly say that it is under God's dominion? Does the world look more like Heaven or the domain of darkness? Obviously, there is darkness in the world, and some people might conclude that Satan is winning—that the world is firmly in his control as it hurls towards the abyss. But they forget that God retains ultimate authority and that He has commissioned us for a specific purpose.

Sure, most Christians believe that Jesus defeated Satan. But they view that victory as a technicality rather than an all-pervasive authority that can permeate our lives and flow out to a lost and oppressed world. Tragically, many Christians have left Jesus' victory on an old rugged cross, giving in to the lie that God plans for the world to keep getting worse until Jesus returns and straightens the whole mess out. Instead, God's plan is clearly laid out in scripture, and while it does not prophesy defeat, neither does it prescribe our passive position in the process.

> But He [Jesus], having offered one sacrifice for sins for all time, sat down at the right hand of God, waiting from that time onward until his enemies be made a footstool for his feet.
>
> Hebrews 10:12-13

Do you see it? Jesus is sitting at the right hand of God the Father, waiting until His enemies are made a footstool! And what does "waiting" mean? Literally: *to wait with expectation, to take or receive from.*

So if Jesus is sitting and waiting, who is God using to make Jesus' enemies a footstool?

Who?

US! That's right us, His people!

As we partner with God, He uses US to restore the Earth just as He intended with Adam and Eve. Man, redeemed through Christ, fulfilling his original commission to subdue the Earth and rule over it, just as God intended all along.

When Jesus gave us the Great Commission, He restored more than the heart of man. He restored man's original calling.

> And Jesus came up and spoke to them, saying, "All authority has been given to Me in heaven and on Earth. Go therefore and make disciples of all the nations, baptizing them in the name of the Father and the Son and the Holy Spirit, teaching them to observe all that I commanded you; and lo, I am with you always, even to the end of the age."
>
> Matthew 28:18-20

Do not mistake the intent of Jesus' words. They are as potent today as they were 2,000 years ago. *"Go therefore..."* is a commission powered by delegated authority. God's authority does not stop with *"All authority has been given to Me..."* Indeed, it only begins there.

As Jesus breathed His life into twelve men, He formed a structure for those who followed to possess His life so that the power and authority of the Kingdom of Heaven could flow to the Earth, restoring what had been lost and establishing what can never be conquered.

Jesus is returning to Earth to receive His kingdom and to complete its full manifestation. He is returning for a victorious church, a mature people, a spotless bride. Together we are preparing the Earth for His coming.

Let's understand how to do this.

Chapter 4

What Did Jesus Say He Would Build?

Jesus lived on Earth during a pivotal time in history. The Greek Empire had recently ended, while the Roman Empire was asserting its dominance over the known civilized world, including the Middle East where Jesus lived. As a result, the people of Jesus' time were strongly influenced by three major cultures: Greek, Roman, and Jewish. It is in this context that we must view Jesus' words, delivered to a wide-eyed group of disciples who often stood in astonishment at the incredible things their Lord shared.

> *Now when Jesus came into the district of Caesarea Philippi, He was asking His disciples, "Who do people say that the Son of Man is?" And they said, "Some say John the Baptist; and others, Elijah; but still others, Jeremiah, or one of the prophets." He said to them, "But who do you say that I am?" Simon Peter answered, "You are the Christ, the Son of the living God." And Jesus said to him, "Blessed are you, Simon Barjona, because flesh and blood did not reveal this to you, but My Father who is in heaven. "I also say to you that you are Peter, and upon this rock <u>I will build My church</u>; and the gates of Hades will not*

> *overpower it. I will give you the keys of the kingdom*
> *of heaven; and whatever you bind on Earth shall*
> *have been bound in heaven, and whatever you loose*
> *on Earth shall have been loosed in heaven."*
>
> Matthew 16:13-19 (underline added)

Notice the underlined words above where Jesus says that He would build His church. The word "church" is the word English translators used for the Greek word *ekklesia*. Jesus is the first and only one who used the word *ekklesia* in all four gospel books. It only appears here in Matthew 16 and twice in Matthew 18.

Consider further that the disciples had never heard the word "church" or been exposed to the concept of what we think of as "church." So would they have had a frame of reference for what Jesus was saying He would build? No. So, since "church" would have been a brand new concept, isn't it interesting that this incessantly inquisitive bunch did not ask Him what He was talking about? Also, if it wasn't church, then what did they relate His words to?

We have the same issue today. When you hear the word "church," what comes to mind? My frame of reference is from my culture and experience, right or wrong. I think of a building with a preacher and God's people in it. I also think of what takes place inside, like singing songs of praise, listening to sermons, and taking an offering or two. The apostles didn't have a frame of reference at all.

We often ascribe meaning to words that our Lord never intended. Indeed, the modern term church evokes many images, most of which are contrary to Jesus' original intent. If you look up the definition of "church," you will get something like this:

> *A building for public worship, especially in the Christian*
> *religion.*

All the followers of a religion, especially the Christian religion, considered collectively.

A religious service that takes place in a church building.

So the modern word "church" can refer to Christians, the building Christians meet in, or the service held in the building where Christians meet. Is this what Jesus intended? Further illumination comes as we carefully examine the original Greek word *ekklesia.*

Ekklesia Word Study

For students of etymology, the study of the origin and history of words, the English word "church" is derived from the Old English word, *cirice*. It is related to words of different languages; Germanic (European) - *kirika*, Old German - *chirihha,* Scottish - *kirk*. All these words that mean church originated from the Greek word *kuriakon*. Interestingly, this Greek word did not exist during the writing of the New Testament. At the time Jesus said, *"I will build My church,"* there was not a word in any language for "church."

The ancient Greek word *kurios* means "lord." This word is used many times in the New Testament. A form of the word *kurios* is *kuriakos*, which means "belongs to the Lord," It is used in the New Testament only two times; in 1 Corinthians 11:20 (the Lord's Supper) and in Revelation 1:10 (the Lord's Day). *Kūriakon* is a late Greek word meaning the "Lord's house." It is this Greek word that the English word church is derived from and its emphasis is more on the building or place where people met and not on the people themselves or their activities. Regardless, during the writing of the New Testament, the word "church" did not exist. "Church" did not become a word until the 4th century, more than 300 years after Jesus had this conversation with His disciples and after Matthew wrote this gospel letter.

However, the English word "church" is in the King James Version (KJV) of the Bible and the New American Standard Bible (NASB) 77 times. (Further in our discussion, we will see how that came to be.) The Greek word *kūriakon* (church) is not the actual word used when the New Testament was written since it did not exist. In the first three centuries, the Greek-speaking people of God would have used the words *Kuriake Oikia* (the Lord's house) to speak of the place, the actual building or location where they met. These would have been the closest words meaning "church" at that time. The Greek word "synagogue" could also have been used, but more specifically, it pertains to a Jewish meeting place, not a Christian meeting place.

While Jesus most likely knew Hebrew, Greek and Latin, He mainly spoke Aramaic—the language of His culture. The Aramaic word *k'nusta* is the word that Jesus would have spoken in Matthew 16 and 18 where the English word "church" is used. Even though Jesus most likely used this Aramaic word when speaking, we know that when Matthew wrote his gospel, he chose to use the Greek word *ekklesia* as the most precise word to describe what Jesus meant.

The Greek word translated as "church" by our English Bible translations is *ekklesia*. *Ekklesia* is derived from two words: *Ek*, which means: *out from among*, and *klesia* which comes from the word *kaleo*, meaning: *to call out*. Together, these words mean: *to call out from among*. The word also means: *an assembly or congregation*. This is a general definition of the word, and unfortunately, it yields little of our Lord's true intent as He spoke to His disciples centuries ago. If we use this definition alone, for example, we have no idea of who assembles and for what purpose.

Ekklesia in Culture

Even though etymology can be helpful when understanding the meaning of a word, it can be somewhat limited because it only examines the origin of a word and its history of usage through the years. Therefore, relying only on etymology is not always the best way to understand a word. Usage, definitions, and connotations of words change with time and cultures. A truer meaning of Jesus' intent comes from studying the cultural context in which *ekklesia* was used.

Ekklesia was a common Greek word used in the time of the New Testament. Both the Greeks and the Romans had an *ekklesia*. So it is likely that the disciples knew exactly what Jesus was saying when He said he would build His *ekklesia*, although they probably did not relate it to a religious organization because *ekklesia* was not strictly a religious term. It was used more in a social and political sense.

The roots of *ekklesia* reach back to the city of Athens during the classical period (550 to 350 BC). Within the Greek city-state *ekklesia* meant a governing body comprised of all male citizens 18 years and older who retained their civil rights. The *ekklesia*'s powers were nearly unlimited. The duties and authority of the *ekklesia* included the following:

> *It elected and dismissed magistrates and directed the policy of the city.*
>
> *It declared war and it made peace.*
>
> *It negotiated and approved treaties and arranged alliances.*
>
> *It chose generals, assigned troops to different campaigns, raised the necessary money, and dispatched those troops from city to city.*

It was an assembly or congregation in which all members had equal right and duty.

This was the common definition of *ekklesia.* As you can see, its primary emphasis was governmental—quite different from church as we know it today.

The fact that ekklesia was a familiar concept in that culture, explains why the disciples didn't ask Jesus questions during this conversation; they already understood what He was saying. You see, the Jews knew that the Messiah was coming to earth, and they were looking for Him. Only, they thought He would come in a different way than He did, and that He would be something different than He was. They also believed that when He came, He would set up His kingdom (government) on earth. So, that day when he spoke of building an ekklesia, it would not have been a surprise when they heard Jesus speaking of building His kingdom government. In fact they asked him several times when He would set up his government/kingdom. Although it may have been a shock when they found out He was leaving the administration of it up to them because He was going to Heaven and would be sending the Holy Spirit to help them.

Jesus' *Ekklesia*

Jesus didn't tell His disciples that He wanted them to join the *ekklesia,* as in something that already existed. Instead, He said that He would "build" one; a new one; His own. It would be used for different purposes than the *ekklesias* of Greece or Rome. Jesus intended to build an assembly belonging to God, assembled for God's purposes; an *ekklesia* to hear from God so that people could speak and act for God. The *ekklesias* of the Greeks and Romans ruled the middle-eastern world for centuries. Jesus intended that His *ekklesia* would establish the Kingdom of God to rule for eternity.

For a child will be born to us, a son will be given to us; and the government will rest on His shoulders; and His name will be called Wonderful Counselor, Mighty God, Eternal Father, Prince of Peace. There will be no end to the increase of His government or of peace, on the throne of David and over his kingdom, to establish it and to uphold it with justice and righteousness from then on and forevermore. The zeal of the Lord of hosts will accomplish this.

Isaiah 9:6-7

Jesus said He now has all authority in Heaven and Earth. He commissioned us to go into all the world to make disciples of all nations. It is the will of God that all nations come to know Christ Jesus and experience the culture of the Kingdom of Heaven now in this age. The previous passage also tells us that there will be no end to the increase of His government. He alone will be Lord and King.

And the Lord will be king over all the Earth; in that day the Lord will be the only one, and His name the only one.

Zechariah 14:9

Naturally, any casual observer of Christianity will immediately recognize the disparity between what Jesus said He would build and the modern church. In the next chapter we will discuss how Christianity went from being the *ekklesia*—the government of the Kingdom of Heaven on Earth with all the authority of Heaven—to what we have today.

(Author's Note: In the following chapters, I will be referring to the church as the *ekklesia*—the term more accurately associated with Jesus' intentions. However, either word will suffice, as long as we understand the meaning behind the words. Our study is not a game of semantics; we are seeking to uncover the full weight and power of Jesus' intent, as revealed by His words.)

Chapter 5

How Did We Get Here?

Have you ever been driving somewhere and realized you were daydreaming the entire time and you could not remember exactly how you got there? You know you drove down certain streets and through traffic lights, but you can't remember whether you actually stopped or not? This has happened to me too many times. I was blindly going through the motions of driving while being unaware of the journey. That's scary!

Just like driving, it is important to know how we—the Body of Christ—got to where we are. An informed historical perspective will help us understand this and not repeat the same mistakes. If we are going to walk with the Lord and be what He created us to be, fulfilling our destiny by accomplishing all He has for us to do on Earth, we must grasp a few fundamental principles.

Let's examine the following:

What were God's original intentions for us?

Who did He create us to be, and what did He create us to accomplish?

Who was Jesus when He lived on Earth, and who are we when we are born again?

In addition to our new nature which we all share in common after we are born again, we also share a common purpose as the people of God. To appreciate this purpose, we must fully comprehend what Jesus said He would build, and grasp the foundation He laid at the onset of building it. Experienced carpenters know that a building's foundation reveals much about the completed, resulting superstructure.

Part of the reason Jesus came to Earth was to lay the foundation for building His *ekklesia*. Many of the things He did were focused on realizing that goal. As we see the foundation that Jesus laid for the establishment of His *ekklesia*, we will have a better picture of how we fit in the plan of God with our individual gifts, talents and callings. So, let's take a look at how Jesus wanted the foundation of His *ekklesia* to be formed.

Jesus and His Apostles

After Jesus' baptism and temptation in the wilderness, He began preaching repentance, for the Kingdom of Heaven was at hand (Matthew 4:17). This is the same message that John the Baptist was preaching prior to Jesus beginning His ministry on Earth. Jesus chose twelve men from all of the others who followed Him to be His closest disciples. Jesus had a few groups of people who followed Him. There were the multitudes, the seventy, the twelve and the three (Peter, James and John). Specifically speaking of the twelve disciples, He taught these men, trained them, equipped them and sent them out to do the work of the Kingdom: healing the sick, casting out demons, proclaiming the Kingdom message and establishing communities of believers.

These twelve disciples that Jesus handpicked, He later named as apostles.

And when day came, He called His disciples to Him and chose twelve of them, whom He also named as apostles.

Luke 6:13

Names and titles are very important to the Lord. Throughout the Bible, God changed people's names for specific purposes. Names describe the identity and purpose of the individual. Titles describe the function. Even the names that Adam gave to all the animals describe the identity of that animal. Function follows identity. A person who works on plumbing is called a plumber. The title "plumber" identifies their function. The title "teacher" identifies a person as one who teaches. When we think of a dog, that term identifies an animal that has certain characteristics and traits. Dogs bark and have four legs and lap water with their tongues. Their identity or nature determines their function. So when we speak of an apostle or a prophet, for example, those titles describe their function.

When Jesus chose His twelve, they were called disciples at first. A disciple is more than one who learns from his teacher. A disciple models his life, behaviors, habits and character after the teacher. Because of this, the disciple has the same general goals and purpose as his teacher. The word disciple is the root word of discipline. A disciple of Jesus is one who is in the process of being disciplined in the ways of Jesus. Like the original disciples before us, each of us who have been born again is to be a disciple of Jesus.

Out of all of Jesus' disciples, it was the twelve to which He also gave the title of apostle, describing their future destiny and function. So the context of the conversation in Matthew 16 about building His *ekklesia* was only with the twelve apostles.

It should be clear by now that Jesus was already forming the foundation of His *ekklesia* by taking twelve disciples, training them to be apostles and teaching them the precepts of the new government of the Kingdom of Heaven on Earth. Like "apostle," *ekklesia* is a name that describes a function. *Ekklesia* is not the Kingdom of Heaven; it is the government of the Kingdom of Heaven. *Ekklesia* describes the function of that government.

Notice that Jesus did not begin building His *ekklesia* with prophets, evangelists, pastors or teachers. He began with apostles. We could consider this the foundational office along with prophets (just below apostles).

> *God's household having been built on the foundation of the apostles and prophets, Christ Jesus Himself being the corner stone.*
>
> Ephesians 2:20

Many today believe that we no longer need apostles; that they were only for establishing the early church. Unfortunately, this is a misunderstanding of scripture, likely coming from the idea that Jesus was building a church. Since Jesus actually said He was building His *ekklesia*—and we are far from realizing that goal—we should see how critical the office of apostle still is today. There is no scriptural evidence to support the belief that the office of apostle is no longer needed. In fact, scripture strongly suggests otherwise, as evidenced below.

> *And He gave some as apostles, and some as prophets, and some as evangelists, and some as pastors and teachers, for the equipping of the saints for the work of service, to the building up of the body of Christ; until we all attain to the unity of the faith, and of the knowledge of the Son of God, to a*

mature man, to the measure of the stature which belongs to the fullness of Christ. As a result, we are no longer to be children, tossed here and there by waves and carried about by every wind of doctrine, by the trickery of men, by craftiness in deceitful scheming; but speaking the truth in love, we are to grow up in all aspects into Him who is the head, even Christ, from whom the whole body, being fitted and held together by what every joint supplies, according to the proper working of each individual part, causes the growth of the body for the building up of itself in love.

Ephesians 4:11-16

This passage makes it clear that Jesus gave these gifts to the Body of Christ for equipping the saints—that's all of us who have been born again—until all attain to the unity of the faith as a mature bride. Since we obviously have not reached this goal, we still need all five gifts. We need apostles. We need prophets. We need evangelists, pastors and teachers. We need all of these gifts—and the others the Bible mentions—working together in unity and harmony.

Of course, we could argue the converse. If apostles have ceased their function, then why not prophets, evangelists, pastors and teachers as well? Well, sure, get rid of the prophets. Not many like them anyway; they can be pretty controversial (just kidding of course). But evangelists? Has the office of evangelist gone away? Nobody to preach the gospel to the lost? What about teachers? Has Jesus said we are done with teachers? Nobody to instruct the Word of God to eager hearers? Who is going to explain this book to the masses? Surely the stupidity of this argument is apparent.

Of course, the one gift that most of us fixate on is that of pastor. Because of this, the office of pastor has been elevated to a level that was never intended. It is the most common and accepted office among the body of Christ today, so much so that we have pastors of nearly everything in our congregations. We have senior pastors, assistant pastors, associate pastors, youth pastors, children's pastors, worship pastors, missions' pastors, outreach pastors, men's group pastors, women's group pastors, even pastor pastors. (I kid not.)

Isn't it interesting that the gift of pastor is only mentioned once in the New Testament, and yet we have thousands of pastors in the world today. But the gift of apostle is mentioned seventy-two times yet there are few who call themselves or are recognized as apostles? There seems to be an imbalance or misunderstanding about this title and its function. But remember what we just saw: Jesus laid the foundation of the *ekklesia* with the apostolic gift. Not evangelists, teachers OR pastors.

Apostle Explained

Assuming I've convinced you that apostles are still needed today, allow me to give a brief overview of the identity and function of an apostle as it pertains to our subject: Jesus' *ekklesia*. (For further study, there are several good books on apostolic ministry.)

The common definition of an apostle is a "sent one," such as a missionary or a messenger. The word "apostle" literally means, "One sent forth with orders." (Like when my wife sends me to the store with a shopping list; I am her apostle, which is the best word I've heard for it in a while.)

"Apostle" is originally a Greek word. The first use of this term was given to a naval commander—one who was in charge of a fleet of ships that were sent out to establish a colony.

In the context of the *ekklesia*, an apostle is first and foremost a military leader for the purpose of advancing the Kingdom of Heaven on Earth. I know that to think of an apostle as a military leader is foreign to many in the church today. This is because we have more of a business mentality than a military or governmental mindset. Of course, I am not advocating that we purchase military fatigues and boots, and start military drills on Sunday morning. Jesus is building His *ekklesia*, not His militia. However, it is interesting to note that God is referred to as "The Lord of Hosts" more often than any other title in the Bible. "Lord of Hosts" literally means "Lord or Commander of an army." An army is under the direct authority of a government. With these terms in mind, let's read Matthew 28:18-20 again.

> And Jesus came up and spoke to them, saying, "All authority has been given to Me in heaven and on Earth. Go therefore and make disciples of all the nations, baptizing them in the name of the Father and the Son and the Holy Spirit, teaching them to observe all that I commanded you; and lo, I am with you always, even to the end of the age."
>
> Matthew 28:18-20

When read with a military or governmental mindset rather than a business mindset, Jesus' words assume a more meaningful purpose. We are told to go into all the Earth to establish a Kingdom of Heaven culture in every nation. This includes transforming the Seven Mountains of Society; religion, government, family, education, arts and entertainment, business, and media.

Notice that we are not told to go into all the Earth and build sheep pens so someone can feed them, nor are we told to plant a church business with programs and social events advertised with creative marketing techniques to provide for people's perceived needs. While there is nothing wrong with programs if they fulfill the purpose of God for making disciples of all nations, cities and people, we need to be clear on our focus. Are we building God's kingdom, or our own? And are we following God's directions for success or the world's?

While it can be easy to confuse the two at times, we need to stay focused on the goals Jesus gave us. To do so, we need the correct gift that He gave the Body of Christ for accomplishing those goals, starting with apostles. Let's remember that Jesus spoke Matthew 28:18-20 specifically to apostles. It will be apostles, prophets and the other five-fold gifts that will lead us in accomplishing the Great Commission. Tragically, many today have rejected these first two gifts which are so desperately needed. Is it any wonder that we struggle to produce real and lasting fruit for the kingdom?

In 1 Corinthians 12:28, Paul gives another list of gifts that God appointed in the *ekklesia*.

> *And God has appointed in the church [ekklesia] first apostles, second prophets, third teachers, then miracles, then gifts of healings, helps, administrations, various kinds of tongues.*
>
> 1 Corinthians 12:28

Notice that this list is written in order of importance with apostles first. Later in verse 31, Paul tells us to desire the greater gifts, referring to the list in verse 28.

In describing the function of an apostle, we notice that they are more governmental in nature. They are equipped to develop an army, training and equipping people to be Christ-like in accomplishing the Great Commission. Of course, the Great Commission is not just for apostles; it is for all of us regardless of our gifts. Therefore, each of us is vital to achieving the goal. We do this by sharing the common thread of apostolic nature woven into our identity, giving us the mindset, ability and authority to accomplish the task Jesus gave us. I call this common thread "apostolic DNA." Every person, regardless of gifts or nature, needs to have apostolic DNA as part of their being.

Sadly, with the over-emphasis of the gift of pastor, the majority of Christians have pastoral DNA to the exclusion of apostolic DNA. The problem with this is that the pastoral gift, although very much needed in the Body of Christ, is not equipped to develop an army by itself, or to take cities, regions, or nations. It is no wonder that pastors are more popular than apostles. The pastoral gift is generally more focused on caring for people: teaching, counseling, working them through relationship issues, and tending to the concerns of a local congregation. While this is needed in the Body of Christ, if that is all we do, we will not accomplish the Great Commission, let alone see our cities and nations transformed. Without apostolic DNA spurring us forward, our local churches can easily devolve into adult daycare centers.

Certainly, any of the other gifts can be over-emphasized. Yet when each of us has apostolic DNA woven into our internal fabric, we not only function stronger in our own gifts, but we will have the same purpose, mindset and authority to function more powerfully in harmony with one another.

God is reclaiming the Earth for His glory, restoring it to His original intent. We have the honor of partnering with Him to accomplish it. According to Acts:

> *Whom heaven must receive until the period of restoration of all things about which God spoke by the mouth of His holy prophets from ancient time.*

> Acts 3:21

Jesus is not building a business where He or anyone else is the Chief Executive Officer (CEO). He is building His government—His *ekklesia*—on Earth as it is in Heaven. It will usher in His Kingdom where He is King. The present age will end, and Jesus will be King over the whole Earth.

> *"As I live," says the Lord, "Every knee shall bow to Me, and every tongue shall give praise to God."*
>
> Romans 14:11

> *So that at the name of Jesus every knee will bow, of those who are in heaven and on earth and under the earth,*
>
> Philippians 2:10

Jesus is the King of His Kingdom that is being established on Earth. Of His reign, there will be no end. This is the direction this age is headed, and it will arrive with the complete manifestation of the Kingdom of Heaven on Earth. Just as Jesus sent out seventy disciples, two by two, to every city to prepare the way for Him (Luke 10:1) we are here on Earth to prepare the way for the second coming of the Lord Jesus. Just as John the Baptist had the spirit of Elijah (Matthew 11:14), and so prepared the way for Jesus' first coming, we are the generation with the spirit of Elijah preparing the way for the Jesus' second coming.

Something Happened Years Ago

From the Book of Acts and the epistles, we gain insight into the formation of the *ekklesia*—it's purpose and the experience of the early Christians. For 300 years after Christ's resurrection, the Body of Christ functioned as an *ekklesia* just as Jesus intended. Apostles, prophets, evangelists, pastors, teachers and disciples spread the Kingdom throughout the known world often facing extreme hardship.

From the Day of Pentecost, we read about the bold and powerful sermons Peter preached and how thousands came to a saving knowledge of Jesus Christ. We read about the miracles believers performed and the persecution they endured. We see the community of believers coming together to worship, pray, share meals and learn from the apostles (Acts 2:42). When a great persecution struck Jerusalem soon after the Day of Pentecost, many Christians fled to other regions. While this may seem like a fear-based retreat, it was actually part of God's plan, resulting in the gospel of the Kingdom spreading to areas never breached by the word of God.

From the Book of Acts, we also see Saul become Paul by being born again, healed of blindness and filled with the Holy Spirit. We read about the missionary journeys of Peter, Paul, Philip, Barnabas, Silas, and the signs, wonders and miracles that flowed from their faith. They preached Jesus and the Kingdom everywhere they went. We see that the gospel of the kingdom was not only for the Jew, but for the Gentile as well. Many were born again, healed, delivered, saved and cleansed.

Throughout this time, apostles established communities— *ekklesias*—of believers with leadership to oversee these congregations in the towns and cities they visited. They took seriously the commission that Jesus gave them, and they followed His mandate for its execution, enduring withering affliction for the cause of Christ.

At the end of these difficult and yet prolific 300 years, something happened that changed everything. Peace was established between the *ekklesia* and its opposition. Upon first glance, this might seem like a victory. We shall see, however, that it had unintended consequences.

In the year 313, the Roman emperor Constantine became a Christian, answering the desperate prayers of generations of believers crushed beneath the boot of Rome's oppression. Newly converted, Constantine promptly legalized Christianity in order to end the persecution of Christians. He further demanded that all seized Christian property be returned. He also called for Christian councils to settle divisive questions on key points of doctrine. The first council convened was the Nicaea Council which, among other things, addressed the identity of Jesus.

While Constantine's benevolence towards Christianity stopped short of establishing it as the official religion, forty years after His death, the emperor Theodosius I did make Christianity the religion of the state in 380 A.D.

Nothing could have been better for Christianity, right?

Well…not so fast.

In the aftermath of the cultural and governmental acceptance, the apostolic *ekklesia* changed, becoming a pastoral church— settled, calm, steady and predictable. In the process, the pioneering spirit was eroded; the clergy was elevated; control of the masses and appeasement of powerful people become the focus; a kingdom mindset became a business mindset. Further, the early believers' identity was stripped of passion and skewed in the direction of abasement and conformity. Predictably, resources now flowed to priests and kings waging wars in the name of God.

As bad as this was, it was also during this time that *ekklesia* was replaced by the word "church." Let's find out how this happened.

The History of "Church"

The English word "church" is used in the Bible 77 times, translated from the Greek word *kūriakon*. But as we discussed earlier, this word didn't exist during the first century when Jesus said He would build His *ekklesia*. So why is it translated as "church" today? As we will see, it was more than just etymology. Something greater was at stake.

William Tyndale was the first person to translate the Bible directly from the Hebrew and Greek texts. Unfortunately, he was not authorized by the king to translate the Bible into English, so he paid dearly for his great work. Beginning in 1525, he finished the entire New Testament and the Pentateuch (the first five books of the Old Testament). His translation of the Bible was also the first to be mass printed using an early printing press. As a result, his Bible translation made it into the hands of the common people, posing a dire threat to the two reigning religious institutions at the time: the Roman Catholic Church and the Church of England (which was controlled by the King of England). Control of scripture was vital to both organizations, as it enabled control of the people.

Of course, had Tyndale stopped there, he might have been all right, but he also included his commentaries with his Bible translations which were considered heresy to both of these powerful churches, thus making him powerful enemies.

One of Tyndale's greatest offenses, however, was his translation of Matthew 16 and 18. Specifically, he did not use the English word "church" that is used today. Instead, he used "congregation."

That's it—"congregation." One little word. One great transgression.

So why was this simple change an affront to the prevailing powers? Because "congregation" refers to the people, not just to leadership. Outside of the purview and control of the rulers, Tyndale's translation—in line with Jesus' intent—told people that they were free to receive Christ and be part of His *ekklesia*, and that they would have authority given by God. They were not the laity to be ruled by a privileged few. By translating the Bible as he did, Tyndale gave the power and authority of God's word into the hands of every Christian rather than merely the Church leaders.

Tyndale's threat to the Roman Catholic Church and the Church of England eventually became too great for these religious establishments to bear, and they reacted as any threatened organization would do—with swift and certain vengeance.

Tyndale was finally arrested by church authorities in 1535, tried and convicted of heresy, and imprisoned for over 500 days in horrible conditions. He was then strangled and burnt at the stake in the prison yard in 1536. His last words on Earth were, *"Lord, open the King of England's eyes."* Tyndale's prayer was answered three years later, resulting in the publication of King Henry VIII's 1539 English Great Bible. Tyndale paid a great price for a great leap forward.

Then in 1604, on the heels of the Great Bible, King James of England also authorized the translation of the Bible into the English language. He chose 47 scholars for the translation work, and while their credentials were impeccable, there was also some bias. For starters, each one of the translators was a member of the Church of England—firmly under the rule and reign of the King. As such, they were under obligation to the King and required to follow his requirements. King James laid out 15 rules for the translators; most of which resulted in excellent scholarship, but at least one revealed an alternative agenda.

Rule three stated:

> *3. The Old Ecclesiastical Words to be kept, viz. the Word Church not to be translated Congregation & c.*

Again, we see a battle over a seemingly insignificant word. Yet King James' seemingly simple requirement was to have profound implications for how we view Jesus' intentions towards His future kingdom government. King James' obvious intent was to consolidate power within enforceable boundaries—the Church of England—and ensure that no other entity could establish a form of government beyond his control. It seemed that King James had not forgotten the transgressions of Tyndale's translation after all, even though James' translators used 90% of Tyndale's translation.

Hence, "church" gave King James a sense of security and control, whereas other translations of *ekklesia*, such as "congregation," "assembly," or worst of all "government," probably threatened him. This *ekklesia* was truly a threat to Satan and the domain of darkness.

The Power of a Word

Words are powerful. John tells us that *In the beginning* started with a Word. King James knew the power of words as well, and just as intended, his manipulation of Jesus' message through the misinterpretation of the one word *ekklesia* changed the course of history. Unfortunately, much harm has come by changing this one word.

In our mis-defining of *ekklesia* as "church," we have misunderstood our full purpose and goal as Christ's body. The corruption of *ekklesia* has led to a mindset that distorted other aspects of Christianity and confused our worldview. This mindset has changed the shape of our gatherings and meetings. It has affected how we interpret scripture. We moved from apostolic leadership to pastoral leadership. We went from developing an army of leaders to merely feeding flocks of sheep. We shifted from occupying the land to mere existence and from dominion to survival—grateful to attend a church where someone will spoon-feed us. We went from meeting the needs of the Lord to meeting the needs of sheep, producing an entitlement mentality living way below the supernatural abundant life that Jesus came to give us.

This church mindset has produced a consumer-based product of watered down goods that requires little to no sacrifice. It has produced a business minded leadership that causes us to mis-define success. We have based success on how *my* business/church is doing and not how the city or region that we have been called to is doing. We fail to assess the most critical judgment to our own existence: is my city or region looking more like the Kingdom of Heaven or the domain of darkness? We have based success on how many people are attending our weekly services, events and programs, and how many people put their names on a salvation card, regardless of whether they have genuinely been born again or only seeking the freebies we hand out.

We applaud ourselves for giving away money, food, clothes, and other freebies without regard for the dignity of others, furthering the entitlement mentality of our society. We have based success on the size of our budgets and buildings, causing us to develop an independent and competitive mindset.

It has changed how we think, how we act, how we pray, how we interpret the Bible and our entire worldview. We have become weak, powerless and lacking authority. Our identity as "soldiers" and "more than conquerors" has eroded. We are convinced the world is going to hell and nothing will change until Jesus returns. So we have agreed to live below what God has called us to, barely hanging on and suffering "with the patience of Job" through whatever life throws at us. We barely get by and live only for the day when Jesus returns and rescues us from our own spiritual mortality.

We have become an inward social club organizing our meetings to please people and not the Lord while the world around us looks increasingly like the domain of darkness. Pastors have become more like CEO's of a business and leaders of social groups, thinking they are fulfilling the call of God.

Why has all this happened?

Because we have believed a lie about who we really are and how we are to function! It has been proven time and time again: repeat a lie often enough and you will begin to believe it.

We have lost our way. We have lost our true identity and therefore our true function, purpose and goal.

But there is great news! It has been 400 years since King James mandated that the word "church" be used in the English Bibles. Just as the Hebrews were in slavery in Egypt and came out of bondage, we are being freed from the bondage of a false identity and coming into a promised land! We are being restored! At this moment, there is a restoration of all things underway (Acts 3:21). We are learning who He created us to be—the governmental authority He has delegated to disciple nations and release a Kingdom culture into the world. Jesus said we can do the works He did and even greater works (John 14:12). God has rescued us from the domain of darkness and transferred us to the Kingdom of His beloved Son (Colossians 1:13). Even though we are on Earth and it is under the influence of darkness, we belong to the Kingdom of Heaven and are to influence Earth by the Kingdom of Light. We are called to be the light of the world and dispel the darkness! We are called and ordained to subdue the Earth and rule over it!

But God, being rich in mercy, because of His great love with which He loved us, even when we were dead in our transgressions, made us alive together with Christ (by grace you have been saved), and raised us up with Him, and seated us with Him in the heavenly places in Christ Jesus, so that in the ages to come He might show the surpassing riches of His grace in kindness toward us in Christ Jesus.

Ephesians 2:4-7

Instead of waiting to go to Heaven we—the *ekklesia*—are already seated with Christ Jesus in heavenly places, giving us a heavenly perspective to bring Heaven to Earth. By understanding what God has done for us and all that belongs to us, we can live in the Kingdom with all the resources of it every day of our lives. Amen!

Furthering our understanding, we can find a pattern for the *ekklesia* given in the Old Testament. It is the pattern that God gave the nation of Israel. Let's look at this pattern and learn what Jesus was speaking of when He said He would build His *ekklesia*.

Chapter 6

The Pattern

The Old Testament contains the pattern for the *ekklesia* that Jesus is building. This should not be surprising, since the Old Testament was written for our instruction as an example to follow.

> *Now these things happened to them as an example, and they were written for our instruction, upon whom the ends of the ages have come.*
>
> 1 Corinthians 10:11

Among its rich and varied contributions, the Old Testament contains types, shadows, illustrations and patterns of what is more fully revealed in the New Testament. This may seem remarkable, even impossible until we consider that everything that exists comes from God who speaks everything into being and holds everything together by His words (Colossians 1:16). So, His very words are the pattern for what they will accomplish.

> *[Priests] who serve a copy and shadow of the heavenly things, just as Moses was warned by God when he was about to erect the tabernacle; for,*

> *"see," he says, "that you make all things according to the pattern which was shown you on the mountain."*
>
> Hebrews 8:5

Jesus said He did not come to abolish the Law but to fulfill it (Matthew 5:17). Therefore, the New Testament is a fulfillment of the Old Testament, including the fulfillment of the *ekklesia*.

The Old Testament contains a pattern for the *ekklesia* that was revealed in the New Testament when Jesus said, *"I will build My ekklesia."* Let's examine the etymology behind the words spoken and discover what they reveal about Jesus' intentions.

Words to Fulfillment

In the Septuagint (LXX), which is the Hebrew text translated into Greek, the Hebrew word *qāhāl* is translated into the Greek word *ekklesia* most of the time. *Qāhāl* is in the Old Testament 123 times. It is translated *ekklēsia* in the LXX 87 times and 36 times to *sunagōgē* or synagogue. Understanding what *qāhāl* and synagogue mean and how they function will give us a better understanding of *ekklesia*.

The Hebrew word *qāhāl* is translated into English as "congregation," "assembly," or "convocation" (a formal assembly of senior church leaders). "Synagogue" is a Greek word that means a bringing together or assembly. It can mean a periodic meeting of the religious community as well as the place of assembly. Synagogue occurs some 200 times in the LXX. Thirty-six times it is the word *qāhāl*, 127 times as *edah*. The Hebrew word *edah*, in its most general definition, is "group" or "congregation." Biblical text consistently distinguishes between *edah* and *qāhāl* in passages like these:

Now if the whole congregation [edah] of Israel commits error and the matter escapes the notice of the assembly [qāhāl], and they commit any of the things which the Lord has commanded not to be done, and they become guilty; when the sin which they have committed becomes known, then the assembly [qāhāl] shall offer a bull of the herd for a sin offering and bring it before the tent of meeting. Then the elders of the congregation [edah] shall lay their hands on the head of the bull before the Lord, and the bull shall be slain before the Lord.

Leviticus 4:13-15

You shall keep it until the fourteenth day of the same month, then the whole assembly [qāhāl] of the congregation [edah] of Israel is to kill it at twilight.

Exodus 12:6

"I was almost in utter ruin in the midst of the assembly [qāhāl] and congregation [edah]."

Proverbs 5:14

Scholars conclude that the *qāhāl* must have been a judicial body composed of representatives of the *edah*. *Qāhāl*, in many contexts, means "an assembly gathered to plan or execute war." It denotes a gathering to judge or deliberate. *Qāhāl* is used for an assembly that God has gathered to hear from God and act for God. A *qāhāl* is a theocratic organizational structure—a form of government that is both legislative and judicial.

A theocracy is a form of government in which a state is understood to be governed by immediate divine guidance, especially a state ruled by clergy or officials who are regarded as divinely guided. This is how God set up the government of the nation of Israel.

The genesis of this appears when Moses' father-in-law, Jethro, came to visit him and advised him to pick able men to help him judge the people (Exodus 18:17-26). Later, in Deuteronomy 16:18, this situation was formalized when God gave the explicit command to "establish judges and officers in your gates." From this pattern, the Sanhedrin was formed. Sanhedrin means "a sitting together" as in a council. It was the legal court of the Jewish nation. In every city of Israel there was a Sanhedrin made up of 23 judges. The Great Sanhedrin was the Supreme Court; it presided in Jerusalem. The Great Sanhedrin was made up of 71 members including the High Priest as president.

The Hebrew word *qāhāl* and the Greek equivalent word *ekklesia* both can refer to a local assembly or the larger assembly as a whole, depending on context. In Matthew 16:18, *ekklesia* is used in reference to the whole assembly. In Matthew 18:17, *ekklesia* is used in reference to the local assembly.

The Hebrew word for synagogue is b*eit knesset. Beit* meaning house and k*nesset* meaning assembly. *Beit knesset* means "house of assembly." *Knesset* comes from the Aramaic word *k'nusta* meaning "assembly." As mentioned earlier, Jesus' native language was Aramaic, so *k'nusta* is the word Jesus used that was translated into Greek as *ekklesia*. Today, the Knesset is the legislative branch of the Israeli government made up of 120 members. This number corresponds to the 120 that were in the upper room waiting for the promise of the Holy Spirit (Acts 1:15).

The Knesset enacts laws, elects the president and prime minister, supervises the work of the government, and reserves the power to remove the President of the State, the State Comptroller from office, and to dissolve itself and call for new elections. The

Knesset can pass any law by a simple majority, even one that might arguably conflict with the basic laws of Israel. The term *knesset* is derived from the ancient Great Assembly or Great Synagogue which according to Jewish tradition was an assembly of 120 scribes, sages, and prophets, ruling during the period from the end of the Biblical prophets (c. 515 BC) to the time of the development of Rabbinic Judaism (c. 600 AD).

What It All Means

The connection between *k'nusta, knesset, synagogue, ekklesia* and *qāhāl* is that they all are governmental in nature. Although *synagogue* is a very similar word to *ekklesia* and would have been a familiar term of the day, it would have been insufficient to define *ekklesia*. *Synagogue* is used strictly in reference to the religion of Judaism where the focus is on teaching the Hebrew Law.

In contrast, *ekklesia* calls out and invites all people from every culture and language to join it by being born again—the focus being on Christ. Therefore, an *ekklesia* refers to the whole of God's people the way some would say *"the Church,"* meaning "all of us." E*kklesia* is also used to speak of a particular congregation in a location: *"The church on the corner."* And finally, *ekklesia* can also mean a specific group from a congregation chosen to make decisions—usually mature elders or leaders—in a similar way we use groups called councils or boards.

Chapter 7

I Will Build My *Ekklesia*

If we are to better understand what Jesus intends to build, we would be well served to examine the gospel in which the teachings appear. As we have discussed previously, the Greek word *ekklesia*—erroneously translated as "church"—first appeared in the New Testament in the Gospel of Matthew, chapters 16 and 18. Matthew's gospel is remarkable in that it is the only one that records the particular conversation Jesus had with His disciples in detail, and it is the only gospel containing the English word "church." (Other books use "church," but Matthew is the only *gospel* that uses it.)

Matthew's perspective is unique; he wrote his gospel in Greek to Jewish Christians. It is also interesting to note that Matthew was probably an educated man and a wealthy man—a government employee and a tax collector. The reason I believe he was an intellectual or educated man is because he knew the Law and has more references to the Law than the other gospel writers. Many everyday Jews did not know the Law and depended upon the Teachers of the Law to explain it to them. Of the original twelve disciples, he was the only government employee called by Jesus as an apostle—proof that Jesus can use anybody. As an early disciple, he possessed a unique vantage point regarding Jesus' intentions for the *ekklesia*.

It is not surprising that Satan would not only twist the truth of *ekklesia* but also distort the truth surrounding the teaching on *ekklesia* that Jesus gave. There are at least six common misconceptions that come from Matthew's two passages on *ekklesia* that need to be addressed. I have already mentioned one, which is the teaching on the *ekklesia* vs. church. The other five teachings pertain to:

- Peter as the rock of the church
- Binding and loosing
- Where two or three are gathered in my name
- If two of you agree on Earth about anything they may ask it shall be done for them
- We should not judge

Caesarea Philippi

Let's begin with the same passage in Matthew that we have been studying.

> Now when Jesus came into the district of Caesarea Philippi, He was asking His disciples, "Who do people say that the Son of Man is?" And they said, "Some say John the Baptist; and others, Elijah; but still others, Jeremiah, or one of the prophets." He said to them, "But who do you say that I am?" Simon Peter answered, "You are the Christ, the Son of the living God." And Jesus said to him, "Blessed are you, Simon Barjona, because flesh and blood did not reveal this to you, but My Father who is in heaven. I also say to you that you are Peter, and upon this rock I will build My church [ekklesia]; and the gates of Hades will not overpower it. I will give you the keys of the kingdom of heaven; and whatever you bind on earth

shall have been bound in heaven, and whatever you
loose on earth shall have been loosed in heaven."

Matthew 16:13-19

Understanding more about the location where Jesus was speaking also helps bring this scripture to light. This conversation between Jesus and His disciples took place at a particularly notorious region known as Caesarea Philippi. It was built and named by Herod Philip the Tetrarch (one of four joint Roman rulers) who enlarged a small town on a plane 1,150 feet above sea level at the base of Mount Hermon. It lies twenty-five miles north of Galilee on snow-capped Mount Hermon. It can be seen on a clear day from as far away as Nazareth, where Jesus grew up.

Today, Caesarea Philippi is located in the Golan Heights near the border of Syria. The area where Jesus and His disciples were standing is now called Banias or Paneas after the Greek god Pan. Today at Banias there is an image illustrating how the Temple of Pan at Caesarea Philippi might have looked during the time Jesus was there.

Despite its dark underpinnings, Caesarea Philippi is a beautiful place with a large underground spring that feeds into the Jordan River. This area has had several names over the centuries, and it is important to some key Biblical events. It was originally known as Baal-Gad, a Canaanite sanctuary of Baal worship. It is believed that Abraham was on top of the mount overlooking this area when God formalized the covenant He made with him, promising that his descendants would possess this land.

On that day the Lord made a covenant with Abram,
saying, "To your descendants I have given this land,
from the river of Egypt as far as the great river, the
river Euphrates: the Kenite and the Kenizzite and the

Kadmonite and the Hittite and the Perizzite and the Rephaim and the Amorite and the Canaanite and the Girgashite and the Jebusite."

Genesis 15:18-21

When Joshua entered the Promised Land and began to conquer it, the area of Caesarea Philippi was as far north as he went. Alexander the Great conquered this region, and it became a place to worship the Greek gods. After this, Rome conquered the area and it became a stronghold for Roman soldiers where Roman gods and idols were worshipped. A temple dedicated to Emperor Augustus Caesar was also built here.

During Jesus' time, the area was known as a place of idol worship. There were incense altars used to worship idols. The false god Pan, who represented all the gods, was worshipped there. Every false god, idol and even a political leader was worshipped there during Jesus' day, making it repulsive to the Hebrews.

The area contained a rock wall over 100 feet high, and in the side of this wall niches were carved out to place idols. There was also a huge cave with a spring at the bottom feeding into the Jordan River. Many believed that Baal and the Asheroth descended into this cave in the winter. They referred to the cave as the "Gate of Hades." Both animal as well as human sacrifice was common there. It was believed that if the carcass of a sacrificed animal sank in the water, it was an acceptable sacrifice; if it floated, it was rejected.

No Jew, especially a rabbi, would go to this place that was considered the most evil and pagan location on the face of the Earth. Yet, Jesus was intentional when He took His disciples on the 25 mile, two day uphill walk to get to this demonic haven. Remarkably, six days after the visit, Jesus was transfigured on Mount Hermon, a peak that overlooks the region. While the word "Hermon" means *anathema*, as in "something cursed, greatly disliked, detested or devoted to destruction."

Who Am I?

With divine irony that can only come from He who holds the world in His hand, Jesus used the backdrop of this nefarious place known for false gods and idol worship to begin a conversation on His identity. *"Who do people say that the Son of man is?"* The term "Son of man" was most telling because the prophet Daniel used it in speaking of the coming Messiah (Daniel 7:13). Incidentally, Jesus used the term to speak of Himself more often than any other term, even more than "Son of God." "Son of man" referred to the identity of Jesus in reference to His humanity. It was a term the Jews would have been familiar with and instantly identified with. (See also Matthew 16:27-28).

After Jesus heard the disciples' response to his query, He asked a more pertinent question (and likely His point all along): *"Who do you say that I am?"* Peter, flush with divine revelation, responds, *"You are the Christ, the Son of the living God."* We know this was divine revelation because of the response Jesus gave to Peter. *"Blessed are you, Simon Barjona, because flesh and blood did not reveal this to you, but My Father who is in heaven."*

Peter's response in identifying Jesus as the Messiah was so profound that Jesus called him blessed. However, to call someone messiah in those days usually didn't mean you were referring to the Son of God. Messiah was a term used for kings, especially those who would bring freedom to people. Today when we speak of the Messiah, we usually use it exclusively for Jesus. But Peter didn't just call Jesus "a" messiah. He called Him "The Messiah, Son of the living God." To call Jesus merely *a* messiah could mean that Jesus was a king, not necessarily *The* King—the appointed and expected One sent from God. The Jews were expecting a messiah from God during this time, and there are many scriptures as well as prophecies that pointed to this truth. So Peter's confession was more than one man's observation; it was a revelation from God the Father revealing the divine truth of Jesus' identity.

Prerequisite Revelation

I do not believe that Jesus would have spoken further about what He was going to build—the *ekklesia*—if the apostles had not demonstrated a true revelation of who He was. The same is true for us. To have a revelation of the true identity of Jesus is foundational for our own identity and the authority He has given us to walk in. True spiritual authority is delegated to us first because we are sons of God, and second based on the function to which God has individually called us. If we do not understand who Jesus truly is, a man dependent on His Heavenly Father, we will not understand who we are as born-again sons of God. We also will not understand the true spiritual authority we have been given. Spiritual authority is inherited from our Father. Just as a king passes his throne to his son, so we inherit delegated authority from our Father in Heaven. We are co-heirs with Jesus Christ, and we know all authority has been given to Him (Matthew 28:18).

The Rock

> "I also say to you that you are Peter, and upon this rock I will build My church..."
>
> Matthew 16:18

Peter is not the rock Jesus said He would build upon. Jesus said, "I say to you that you are Peter." Then He said, "and upon this rock I will build My church." When He said, "you are" and then in the same sentence, "upon this," it is obvious He was speaking of two different things. We also must remember that Jesus was speaking Aramaic, not Greek what Matthew used to write his gospel. In Greek, Peter is the word *Petros,* meaning a small rock or stone. The word for rock is *petra* which means a large rock or bedrock, a foundational rock. *Petros* is a masculine word and *petra* is a feminine word. Jesus would not have used a feminine word to refer to Peter since he was a male. So even in Greek, it is obvious that Jesus was not calling Peter the rock on which He would build. In Aramaic, the word for Peter is *kêpā (Cephas)* and it is the same word for rock. So Jesus would have said: *"I say to you that you are kêpā (Cephas) and upon this kêpā I will build My k'nusta."* All Jesus did was use a play on words. He was not calling Peter *the* rock He would build on.

There is also a misunderstanding about when Jesus changed Peter's name from Simon to Peter. Many think it was during this conversation but it was not. Jesus changed his name from Simon to Peter when He first met him (John 1:42).

The word rock speaks to several things; the first is the solid rock of revelation that Jesus is the Messiah, the Son of the living God, just as Peter uttered it. In this sense, Peter represents all of God's people with the same revelation. We are all rocks—living stones being built together—all having a revelation that Jesus is the Messiah, Son of God.

> *You also, as living stones, are being built up as a spiritual house for a holy priesthood, to offer up spiritual sacrifices acceptable to God through Jesus Christ.*
>
> 1 Peter 2:5

> *In whom the whole building, being fitted together, is growing into a holy temple in the Lord, in whom you also are being built together into a dwelling of God in the Spirit.*
>
> Ephesians 2:21-22

Rock was also a convenient illustration since Jesus was standing near the 100 foot wall of rock where idols and gods were worshipped. He could not have drawn a more stark contrast between himself and the seat of evil for that region. Jesus was also referring to Old Testament prophecy. In the dream that Daniel interpreted for Nebuchadnezzar, a stone was cut out of the mountain without hands and crushed all the other kingdoms and it became a great mountain and filled the whole Earth. That stone, or rock, represented the Kingdom of Heaven.

> *"You, O king, were looking and behold, there was a single great statue; that statue, which was large and of extraordinary splendor, was standing in front of you, and its appearance was awesome. The head of that statue was made of fine gold, its breast and its arms of silver, its belly and its thighs of bronze, its legs of iron, its feet partly of iron and partly of clay. You continued looking until a stone was cut out without hands, and it struck the statue on its feet of iron and clay and crushed them. Then the iron, the clay, the bronze, the silver and the gold were crushed all at the same time and became like cha from the summer threshing floors; and the wind carried them away so that not a trace of them was found. But the stone that struck the statue became a great mountain and filled the whole earth.*
>
> Daniel 2:31-35

> *"In the days of those kings the God of heaven will set up a kingdom which will never be destroyed, and that kingdom will not be left for another people; it*

will crush and put an end to all these kingdoms, but it will itself endure forever. In as much as you saw that a stone was cut out of the mountain without hands and that it crushed the iron, the bronze, the clay, the silver and the gold, the great God has made known to the king what will take place in the future; so the dream is true and its interpretation is trustworthy."

Daniel 2:44-45

There are many references throughout the Old Testament of God referring to Himself as Israel's rock. The disciples would have been familiar with this image. In light of Peter's revelation of who Jesus was, and from hearing Jesus speak of Himself as a rock, they may have begun to understand that Jesus was the Messiah, Son of God.

Jesus is also referred to as the cornerstone. In the building trades, a cornerstone has precise angles, is perfectly square, and bears the weight of the entire building. All the other stones are laid in place precisely in relationship to the cornerstone. This solid rock foundation is the basis for the *ekklesia*, the government of the Kingdom of Heaven on Earth.

For this is contained in scripture: "Behold, I lay in Zion a choice stone, a precious corner stone, and he who believes in Him will not be disappointed."

1 Peter 2:6

Finally, lest any miss the more obscure references, Jesus made it blatantly plain in Matthew 7:24 when He said that if anyone would hear and act on His words of truth, that man would be like a wise man who built his house on the rock; and when the storms of life came it would not fall because it was founded on *the* rock.

Gates of Hades

At the end of His declaration acknowledging Peter's revelation, Jesus added a statement that could seem to be boastful or even foolishly assertive except for the fact that He was the son of God.

I will build My church, and the gates of Hades will not overpower it.

Matthew 16:18

Gates are entry or exit points to something; in this case, to Hades (Hell)—the place of the dead. The gates of Hell represent the power of death and the domain of darkness. As mentioned, in the spiritually wicked Caesarea Philippi where Jesus and His disciples were standing when Jesus said this, there is a large cave called "the Gates of Hades." It was here at this portal to Hell that animal sacrifice was performed. The Gates of Hell represented all the power of Hell—which ultimately is death. The Kingdom of Heaven represents life and all the protection and provisions God has for us. Again, Jesus was drawing a clear distinction for His disciples.

In addition to entrance and exit places, gates in ancient times stood for authority. Many cities had high walls around them for protection. To access the city you entered through a gate. Large cities had several gates at different parts of the wall. Gates of a city were gathering places. City markets operated near the gates to attract a steady flow of customers. Prophets made their proclamations at city gates where all would hear. The Bible also refers to men sitting at the gates of the city as judges. Courts of law were held at the gates, where elders rendered judgments on civil cases. People often gathered at the city gates to discuss city policy and law—what they would allow or disallow in the city. Thus, the framework for society was established at the gates.

It is within this cultural paradigm that Jesus boldly declared that His *ekklesia*—His Kingdom government—would rule and reign over all of Hell. Furthermore, the *ekklesia* would release life and determine the societal framework in cities, regions and nations. Arrayed against Hell's desires for the destruction of the Kingdom of Heaven on Earth, Jesus said that the *ekklesia*—not the church—would overpower it.

For this, He gave us the keys of the kingdom to use!

Keys to Bind and Loose

> *"I will give you the keys of the kingdom of heaven, and whatever you bind on earth shall have been bound in heaven, and whatever you loose on earth shall have been loosed in heaven."*
>
> Matthew 16:19

Today many US cities honor outstanding civic contributions by giving a person a symbolic "key to the city" signifying great honor and rights to access the offices of civic leaders. In antiquity, it was a common idea that Heaven, as well as Hell, was closed off by doors or gates with locks that only certain gods or angels had the keys to open. This passage from the book of Job, the oldest book of the Bible, speaks of gates to death or hell.

> *Have the gates of death been revealed to you, or have you seen the gates of deep darkness?*
>
> Job 38:17

Remember also that the location of Caesarea Philippi housed what was believed to be the gate of Hades. Jesus used these "Gates of Hades" as an example in His teaching. In Revelation 1:8 Jesus said He has the keys to death and Hades.

This is the context in which Jesus said He would give us keys of the Kingdom of Heaven—keys used to bind and loose. The actual words "bind" and "loose" are legal terms used in the sense of making a contract either legally binding or legally dissolved. This is the binding and loosing process Jesus talked about in both Matthew 16 and 18.

The chief error arising from these passages comes from the teaching that binding and loosing are used to bind demons and loose angels. In some circles, people are taught to say: *"I bind you Satan in the name of Jesus"* or *"I loose angels to accomplish...."* The problem with this approach is that it takes Jesus' words out of context and is therefore an incorrect teaching. No scripture speaks of binding and loosing in this manner. If this manner of control over demons and angels was a valid teaching, Jesus would have applied it Himself as well as the first disciples and apostles; however, we see no examples of it or teaching about it in scripture.

Spiritual Warfare

The correct Biblical way to bind Satan in our life is by being obedient to the Father as Jesus was. His wilderness temptation is a great example (Matthew 4). Jesus lived a life of obedience to the Father. As such, He was a man of godly character. Possessing the same type of character as Jesus is our greatest defense in spiritual warfare. Indeed, the armor of God includes character traits. When tempted, Jesus spoke the Word of God. Satan has no defense for this type of life; he is bound. After the temptation in the wilderness, the Bible says that Satan left Jesus until a more opportune time. James 4:7 puts it more succinctly:

> *Submit therefore to God. Resist the devil and he will*
> *flee from you.*
>
> James 4:7

Often people try to resist the devil but forget the first part of this scripture: *submit to God.* The more we grow in our relationship with the Lord, acquiring a Christ-like character, the less access Satan has to our life. We bind him with the godly quality of our life.

Strange as it may seem, God actually gave Satan food to eat and a place to live as part of his legal rights. During God's judgment in the Garden of Eden (Genesis 3), He told the serpent that he would eat dust. Dust is dirt, and dirt is what all men are made from, so it also represents the flesh. The flesh is also an idiom for behaving in a carnal or fleshly way (see Galatians 5 the works of the flesh). It is the unregenerate aspect of our nature. So when we act in the flesh, we are giving the demonic realm food that is legally theirs from God. And we all know what happens when you feed something. It grows, and just like a stray dog, it will come back for more or won't leave until the food disappears.

So where does Satan live? In the book of Jude and 2 Peter 2:4 it says that Satan has been chained in darkness. This doesn't mean that he is bound up in a place of darkness. It means he is bound to darkness. Darkness is the realm that God gave Satan as his legal dwelling place. In contrast, Jesus said that we are the light of the world and that a light should not, and in fact could not, be hidden. When we choose to live by darkness and not by the Light, and when we hide things in the dark places of our heart—secret sins and unhealed wounds—we allow Satan access to dwell in those places. He soon becomes the unintended guest who sets up permanent residence in our unlighted abode. Spiritual warfare, in its simplest state, denies the enemy the sustenance and habitation that is legally his.

Kingdom Keys

A key is a symbol of power and authority. When you have the key to a lock, you have the power to either deny or allow access to whatever is kept secure by the lock. For Christians—members of the *ekklesia*—simply knowing God's will in a situation is a key. When we speak and act on the will of God, we release His will on Earth. Of course, a key must be used correctly in order to be effective. To know how to use God's keys, we must know His voice. When we accurately hear from the Lord concerning His will, we receive a key of His Kingdom. What we do with those keys determines whether or not the will of God is accomplished.

An example of using a key is speaking words given by the Holy Spirit through a prophetic decree. This could also be called legislating the will of God. When we do this, we use the key (the message) to either lock (bind) or unlock (loose) spiritual forces that have a direct bearing on natural forces and events. When we faithfully legislate God's will, we accurately hear from God and come into agreement with Him. That agreement, when prophesied, makes the will of God legally binding on Earth, or it has the authority to break (loose) a previously made agreement. For example, when the blood of Jesus was shed, mankind was loosed (freed) from the Old Covenant, and the New Covenant became binding. But the application goes far beyond salvation. There are many legally binding agreements that have been made by the words and actions of men that have not been the will of God: abortion, redefining of marriage, generational curses and slavery are just a few examples. These must be broken through the process we are discussing.

When Jesus gave us keys, He gave us power and authority to accomplish the will of God, as it is in Heaven, on Earth. When used correctly, the keys have potential to advance the purposes of the Kingdom of Heaven as well as stop the advancement of the domain of darkness.

Keys can be either words or actions or a combination of both. Words are powerful! Spoken words inspired by the Holy Spirit have power and authority. God spoke the world into existence. Out of nothing, He created something by the words He spoke! When we speak divinely inspired words, they have the same power and authority as if they were spoken by God Himself.

A divinely inspired act is just as powerful as words. An example is the crucifixion of Christ. The greatest victory ever won was accomplished without a word spoken. Amazing!

The purpose of the *ekklesia* is to accomplish the will of God on the Earth. This is why, when Jesus taught on prayer in Matthew 6:10, He said to pray in this way: *"Your kingdom come. Your will be done, on earth as it is in heaven."* The *ekklesia* is the government of the Kingdom of Heaven on Earth created for the purpose of establishing a kingdom culture in every nation and sphere of society. The keys that Jesus gave us have the power to make or break legally binding agreements. However, given such great power, we must be careful that we are not praying or prophesying according to our own desires and human reasoning, but are hearing accurately from the Holy Spirit.

House of Prayer

When Jesus entered the temple and cleared it of the buyers and sellers as well as the moneychangers, He said,

> *"Is it not written, 'My house shall be called a house of prayer for all nations'? But you have made it a robbers den."*
>
> Mark 11:17

Prayer is communication with the Lord. It is not just a time when we do all the talking; it requires both speaking and listening. For the ekklesia to function correctly, we must be listening and learn to hear and recognize the voice of the Lord, and then say what He is telling us to say and/or do what He is showing us to do. The fundamental principle to ekklesia is illustrated when Jesus told Peter that "flesh and blood did not reveal this to you, but My Father who is in heaven." In other words hearing the revelation like Peter did. Part of the ekklesia's purpose is to release or legislate the will of God on the earth, not our own will or desires, and this is often heard in prayer. But if we are always talking and not listening, we will miss God's voice. Too often we pray our own desires, what we want to see happen, and it may or may not be the will of God. We make many assumptions in prayer and what we think the will of God is, that's why hearing and recognizing the voice of God is critical.

The Government Will Rest On His Shoulders

For a child will be born to us, a son will be given to us; and the government will rest on His shoulders; and His name will be called Wonderful Counselor, Mighty God, Eternal Father, Prince of Peace.

Isaiah 9:6

Isaiah declares that the government rests on the shoulders of Jesus. He is the head and all those who are born again make up the Body of Christ from the shoulders down to the feet. His government rests on His body which resides on the Earth. As Head, He communicates His will to us so we can legislate it and act on it, implementing His will on Earth.

We were made to rule and reign over the Earth with Christ As such, we can change our cities, regions and nations. We do not have to sit back and allow evil to run rampant. In fact, to do so would make us negligent of our God-given responsibility. We should be determining what society looks like. Indeed, we are commanded to do so.

So that the manifold wisdom of God might now be made known through the church [ekklesia] to the rulers and the authorities in the heavenly places.

Ephesians 3:10

In the next chapter, we will focus on one particular key, which is not only a key in the sense of binding and loosing, but one of honor.

Chapter 8

The Key of David

The term "key of David" has been spoken of frequently in recent history. Let's examine its origins in scripture and understand how it applies to today's *ekklesia*.

There are only two scriptures in the Bible with direct references to the key of David. One is Isaiah 22:22 and the other is Revelation 3:7.

> *"Then I will set the key of the house of David on his shoulder, when he opens no one will shut, when he shuts no one will open.*

> Isaiah 22:22

> *"And to the angel of the church in Philadelphia write: He who is holy, who is true, who has the key of David, who opens and no one will shut, and who shuts and no one opens..."*

> Revelation 3:7

The first passage, Isaiah 22:15-25, contains the story of Shebna who was a royal steward (treasurer) of the palace during the reign of Hezekiah. He occupied a high office with great responsibility.

> Thus says the Lord God of hosts, "Come, go to this steward, to Shebna, who is in charge of the royal household, 'What right do you have here, and whom do you have here, that you have hewn a tomb for yourself here, you who hew a tomb on the height, you who carve a resting place for yourself in the rock? Behold, the Lord is about to hurl you headlong, O man. And He is about to grasp you firmly and roll you tightly like a ball, to be cast into a vast country; there you will die and there your splendid chariots will be, you shame of your master's house.' I will depose you from your office, and I will pull you down from your station. Then it will come about in that day, that I will summon My servant Eliakim the son of Hilkiah, and I will clothe him with your tunic and tie your sash securely about him. I will entrust him with your authority, and he will become a father to the inhabitants of Jerusalem and to the house of Judah. "Then I will set the key of the house of David on his shoulder, when he opens no one will shut, when he shuts no one will open. I will drive him like a peg in a firm place, and he will become a throne of glory to his father's house. So they will hang on him all the glory of his father's house, offspring and issue, all the least of vessels, from bowls to all the jars. In that day," declares the Lord of hosts, "the peg driven in a firm place will give way; it will even break off and fall, and the load hanging on it will be cut off, for the Lord has spoken."

> Isaiah 22:15-25

We are not told everything about Shebna. However, in verse sixteen we are given a glimpse into his character. It was a common practice for those of high rank to be buried in a large, beautiful tomb or vault in a place of honor. Shebna was preparing such a place of honor, building a name for himself to be honored after he died. He was focused on himself and leaving a legacy. Shebna was obviously a prideful man. In verses 19 and 20 we are told that God removed him from his office because of pride and replaced him with a man named Eliakim. Then in verse 22, we read that the Lord will *"set the key of the house of David on his [Eliakim's] shoulder."* Note that in this passage the key of David is referred to specifically as *"the key of the house of David."* The Lord is the One who associated this key with the name of David. Jesus, in Revelation 3:7, also referred to this key, calling it simply the key of David.

So why is David's name associated with this key? I believe the answer has everything to do with who David was and the type of character he had.

David was far from a perfect man. None of us are. However, David excelled at proving it. Among other things, he committed adultery and then murdered to cover it up. It is interesting, however, that when most people think of David, they do not remember him for his failures and sins even though the Bible recorded them for every generation to see. Instead, we usually remember David for the quality of man he was: a son, a shepherd, a worshipper, a servant, a father, a warrior and a king. We remember him as the Lord does, as recorded in Acts.

> *After He had removed him, He raised up David to be their king, concerning whom He also testified and said, 'I have found David the son of Jesse, a*

man after My heart, who will do all My will.'

Acts 13:22

Despite his flaws, God calls David a man after His own heart; this is how he is most often remembered. God also says of David that he *"will do all My will."* David was humble and obedient to the Lord even though he sinned. When he did fail—and he failed spectacularly—David humbled himself before God and repented, finding the mercy of God in forgiveness and the grace to carry on.

This reveals the cornerstone of the key of David—it is the heart of David modeled on the heart of Christ. In terms of love, obedience and passion for God, David was a man of Christ-like character.

We see the same heart in the man who replaced the prideful Shebna. To possess the key of David from the Lord required a heart like Eliakim's. When God gave the key of the house of David to Eliakim, whose name means "resurrection of God" or "whom God will raise up," He referred to Eliakim as, *"My servant Eliakim,"* implying that he was a good and faithful man—God's servant.

We also know from Revelation 3:7 that Jesus, who was perfect in character, possessed this key as well. In Revelation 19:11 Jesus is called "Faithful and True." Let's look at just a couple more examples at the type of man that David was.

The central theme of the Bible is God dwelling with us. Jesus came to Earth as Immanuel—God with us. Psalm 132 says that David would not rest until he found a dwelling place for the Lord.

Remember, O Lord, on David's behalf, all his affliction how he swore to the Lord and vowed to the Mighty One of Jacob, "Surely I will not enter my house, nor lie on my bed; I will not give sleep to my eyes or slumber to my eyelids, until I find a place for the Lord, a dwelling place for the Mighty One of Jacob."

Psalm 132:1-5

From the dawn of Earth's creation, God's purpose has always been to dwell with man: mind, body and spirit. This is why, when we are born again, the Spirit of Christ comes to dwell in us. Colossians 1:27 speaks of *"Christ in you the hope of glory."* There can be no greater unity than God living in us, and no greater joy for God than to be with us.

This is why the culmination of the age and all of human history is focused on Jesus' return to Earth. The full manifestation of the Kingdom of Heaven on Earth will be realized in God dwelling with us and Immanuel as King. You see, wherever the King is, there is the Kingdom. All of the resources of the Kingdom are manifest and available wherever the King is present. So if Christ is dwelling in us, then all of the resources of His Kingdom are as well! 2 Peter 1:3 says that He has already given us everything that pertains to life and godliness.

We see the same passion for unity with God in the life of David. Not only was he a humble man after the heart of God, but David was also a warrior who conquered cities and nations to unify the kingdom. The first thing David did when he recaptured Jerusalem was to bring the Ark of the Covenant—signifying the presence of God—back to its rightful place (2 Samuel 6, 2 Chronicles 16). He then established night and day worship, continually ministering to the Lord as the heartbeat of his earthly kingdom.

As a result of David's intentional pursuit of unity with God, 1 Chronicles 18 and 2 Samuel 8 tells us that *"the LORD helped David wherever he went."* David put the Lord first and God was with him, giving him success.

God desires that we have a heart as David's—united with God—so that we walk in the authority that David had. Jesus, in the generational line of David, links those under the Old Covenant with those under the New Covenant, both Jew and Gentile alike. We are to be transformed into His image, possessing the character of Christ so we can walk in His authority. Jesus is our example of who we are, how we are to live and what we must accomplish.

The Key of David is summed up in the heart and identity of David, first as a son, then as a shepherd, a worshipper, a servant, a father, a warrior and a king. It is important that we understand son-ship and biblical adoption especially in our discussion of keys of the Kingdom and the importance of character and unity. As we discussed in the beginning of this book, all who are born again become sons of God. Sons legally inherit the right to the throne from their Father the King.

The Lord desires to partner with us to accomplish His will on the Earth and to accomplish his long-range plan of the full reign of His Kingdom with Jesus as King on the Earth. In 2 Samuel 8 we read.

> *So David reigned over all Israel; and David administered justice and righteousness for all his people.*
>
> 2 Samuel 8:15

Those whose hearts are aligned with the Lord will possess the key of David to further the Kingdom. Obtaining Christ-like character must be a priority for all children of God; it is a requirement for functioning within the *ekklesia*. The Father is looking for those who have a heart of humility, obedience, service and worship. Releasing righteousness and justice is the purpose of the government of the Kingdom of Heaven. Those with a heart for the Father can be trusted with the keys of the Kingdom.

> *Righteousness and justice are the foundation of His throne.*
>
> Psalm 97:2

Delegated Authority

The key of David is a symbol of the power and authority delegated by David over his kingdom in righteousness and justice. Keys are given only to those who are trustworthy. Shebna was lacking in character as noted by his pride, and therefore he lost his position to a man of character—Eliakim. The qualifications for delegation are vital, for the keys are powerful.

In the passage of Revelation 3:7 where Jesus said He is the One that has the key of David, He continues: *"who opens and no one will shut, and who shuts and no one opens."* The key of David, in the hands of the Lord's faithful servants, will have the power and authority to open doors that no one will be able to shut and shut doors that no one will be able to open. As heir to the throne of David, Jesus has all the power and authority of the Kingdom of Heaven. He also has keys to delegate to His faithful servants (Matthew 16:19).

In ancient times, the master servant possessed the keys to all the doors and/or gates of his master's house, much like a janitor in a school does today. These keys would hang around the servant's neck, resting on his shoulders. These trustworthy servants would have full authorization to access the entire house and be able to allow access or deny access to others. Now notice in Isaiah 9:6 that the government rests on Jesus' shoulders, a clear connection between the government of the Kingdom and the keys of the

Kingdom, similar to Matthew 16:19. Isaiah 9 further connects Jesus and His government of the Kingdom of Heaven with David and his earthly kingdom in Israel. It also speaks of a never-ending increase or vastness of the Lord's government that will be established with justice and righteousness.

> *For a child will be born to us, a son will be given to us; and the government will rest on His shoulders; and His name will be called Wonderful Counselor, Mighty God, Eternal Father, Prince of Peace. There will be no end to the increase of His government or of peace, on the throne of David and over his kingdom, to establish it and to uphold it with justice and righteousness From then on and forevermore. The zeal of the Lord of hosts will accomplish this.*
>
> Isaiah 9:6-7

David—Son of God

The kingdom of David is an example of the government of the Kingdom of Heaven on Earth. It is a pattern for us to follow in the present day Kingdom of Heaven. We see in the Bible a continuing truth from the Book of Genesis in the Old Covenant to the Book of Revelation in the New Covenant, that the will of God is for His Kingdom rule to be over the Earth.

As I mentioned in the last section, understanding son-ship is vital to the *ekklesia* for several reasons. One reason is inheritance rights. Only sons have a legitimate right to become kings. Sons inherit the right to rule and reign from their fathers. David had a legal right given to him by God to rule as king because David was a son of God. Then Solomon, as King David's son, inherited the legal right to succeed his father as king. Jesus' reign followed the same pattern. From Hebrews:

For to which of the angels did He ever say, "You are My Son, today I have begotten You"? And again, "I will be a Father to Him and He shall be a Son to Me"?

Hebrews 1:5

This scripture speaks of Jesus and contains two quotes from Old Testament passages. *"You are My Son, today I have begotten You"* is a quote from the Psalms:

"I will surely tell of the decree of the Lord: He said to Me, 'You are My Son, today I have begotten You.'"

Psalm 2:7

The passage is speaking of Jesus. However, the second part of this passage: *"I will be a Father to Him and He shall be a Son to Me,"* is a quote from the Davidic Covenant in 2 Samuel 7:14 and 1 Chronicles 17:13.

"I will be a father to him and he will be a son to Me...."

2 Samuel 7:14

"I will be his father and he shall be My son; and I will not take, My loving kindness away from him, as I took it from him who was before you."

1 Chronicles 17:13

Both of these Old Testament scriptures are speaking of David's son Solomon. So we see that Hebrews 1:5 is saying the same thing about Jesus as Solomon. By combining these verses in speaking of Jesus, the Lord is revealing a twofold purpose: His adoption of David, giving him a legitimate and legal right to rule and that Jesus is actually the Son of God by birth in the line of David. So David was a son by adoption and Jesus by birth. Today, Christians are both birthed and adopted as sons of God; we have inherited the legitimate right to rule as kings. This is our legitimate right to rule as the *ekklesia* in the pattern of David and Jesus.

Inheritance

Romans 8:17 tells us that we are co-heirs with Jesus Christ. As sons of God, we also have legally inherited the right to be priests and kings. Jesus was born in the natural according to the generational line of David through Mary and Joseph (Luke 2:4). Beginning with David, then Solomon, and down to Jesus, all had a legitimate and legal right to reign as kings because of their bloodline.

> *Concerning His Son, who was born of a descendant of David according to the flesh, who was declared the Son of God with power by the resurrection from the dead, according to the Spirit of holiness, Jesus Christ our Lord,*
>
> Romans 1:3-4

There is much to say about the inheritance we receive from the Lord. In keeping with our topic on inheriting the legitimate right to rule and reign as kings on the Earth, let's continue with verse 8 from Psalm 2, where God says to ask for nations as part of our inheritance.

> *Ask of Me, and I will surely give the nations as Your inheritance, and the very ends of the Earth as Your possession.*
>
> Psalm 2:8

As we discussed from Psalm 2:7, this passage is also speaking in reference to Jesus in the line with the Davidic Covenant. Part of God's decree to us is to ask for the nations as our inheritance, and He promises to give them to us as our possession. As kings, we are commissioned with establishing and increasing the Kingdom of Heaven on Earth. The significance in our Father and son relationship with the Lord is seen by the inheritance given. As this age comes to a close and Jesus returns to Earth, we will see every nation, tribe and tongue come under the Lordship of Christ. It is the *ekklesia*'s responsibility to usher in that age.

Restoring the Tabernacle of David

In Acts 15, Paul and Barnabas were in Antioch sharing with the believers about the Gentiles who were born gain and filled with the Holy Spirit. The possibility of Gentiles being born again and filled with the Holy Spirit was a new concept that began with the vision that Peter had in Acts 10:10, where the Lord commanded him to not exclude the Gentiles. Prior to this, the common understanding was that salvation was only for the Jews. So Paul and Barnabas went to Jerusalem to report to the resident apostles what God had done. While they were meeting together, some Pharisees who also believed in Jesus were saying that the Gentiles must be circumcised and obey the Law of Moses. This caused great debate and strife between Paul, Barnabas and these men (not to mention the Gentiles who did not relish the thought of coming under the circumcision knife in the hands of a rabbi).

A meeting concluded with James, who was the apostle of Jerusalem, giving the final judgment on the matter. While speaking in favor of Gentile inclusion in the Body of Christ without demanding they be circumcised, he referred to a prophecy in the book of Amos 9:11-12 that speaks of the rebuilding of the Tabernacle of David so that all of mankind, including Gentiles may seek the Lord. The passage in Amos says:

*"In that day I will raise up the fallen booth of David,
And wall up its breaches; I will also raise up its ruins
And rebuild it as in the days of old; that they may
possess the remnant of Edom and all the nations
who are called by My name," declares the Lord who
does this.*

Amos 9:11-12

Edom in this passage means all the nations that were enemies of Israel--in-other words, Gentile nations.

The account of James' words is recorded in Acts:

*After they had stopped speaking, James answered,
saying, "Brethren, listen to me. Simeon has related
how God first concerned Himself about taking from
among the Gentiles a people for His name. With this
the words of the Prophets agree, just as it is written,
'After these things I will return, and I will rebuild the
tabernacle of David which has fallen, and I will
rebuild its ruins, and I will restore it, so that the rest
of mankind may seek the Lord, and all the gentiles
who are called by My name,' says the Lord, who
makes these things known from long ago. "*

Acts 15:13-18

It is interesting that James used this passage of scripture to prove that Gentiles should be included in the Body of Christ. By combining this scripture with current events during his time, James was saying that the time had now come when the Tabernacle of David was to be restored.

What is the Tabernacle of David? A tabernacle is a tent or a dwelling. The Tabernacle of David, therefore, would be the dwelling of David or the realm over which David is king. It is also referred to as the House of David. Since David ruled over all Israel, the Tabernacle of David is Israel. With this understanding, these two passages show that the work of the *ekklesia* is to restore the house of David, not replace it. God's plan is for the Tabernacle of David to be restored with Jesus as the final King; Jesus as heir to the throne over all the Earth. This is the restoration process that began nearly 2,000 years ago and will culminate at the second coming of Jesus. The Lord is using His *ekklesia* to accomplish His ultimate will for the destiny of the world.

And we hold the key.

Chapter 9

The Branches of *Ekklesia*

As the government of the Kingdom of Heaven on Earth, the *ekklesia* has three distinct branches:

- *the judicial branch*
- *the legislative branch*
- *the executive branch*

The prophet Isaiah illustrated the same in his description of the Lord.

> *For the Lord is our judge, the Lord is our lawgiver, the Lord is our king; He will save us.*
>
> Isaiah 33:22

Notice the parallels:

- *the judicial branch—our judge*
- *the legislative branch—our lawgiver*
- *the executive branch—our king*

The government of the United States of America is also formed from this biblical pattern. However, instead of an elected President, the executive branch of the *ekklesia* is occupied by Jesus. And in place of Congress and the Supreme Court, the legislative and judicial branches of the *ekklesia* are occupied by the people of God. (That would be us.)

These three branches of the *ekklesia* also relate to the Trinity. The Father is the Great Judge, the Son Jesus is the King, and the Holy Spirit is the Lawgiver, or in other words, the One who delivers/ speaks the will of God to us so that we can speak and act on it. Also known as our Helper, the Holy Spirit helps us to legislate and judge according to the will of God.

The Legislative Branch

Legislation is the process of writing and passing laws. Legislation also means the actual law itself. We have already discussed the legislative branch of the *ekklesia* throughout this book, though not in these terms. The responsibility of the legislative branch is to hear from God, then speak and act for God, thereby releasing His will on Earth. God gave man authority over the Earth. For His will to be accomplished, we must hear accurately from Him so that we can implement His will. Of course, we are not there yet, because God's will is not always accomplished. We can easily see that by what is going on in the world today. Although God is in ultimate control, we are the ambassadors He uses to carry out His will on Earth (2 Corinthians 5:20). If God's will is not accomplished, we need look no further than ourselves—His *ekklesia*.

Even as I write this, I realize that some Christians get nervous when speaking of government, politics and especially law in relation to God. Please understand that I am not referring to Old Testament law versus New Testament law, or debating whether we are under law or not. Instead, I am using God's "will" and His "law" interchangeably. In the Kingdom of Heaven, God's will—His law— will always be accomplished. He is the King and the overarching law of the Kingdom, on Earth and in Heaven, is love. Romans 13:10 says that love is the fulfillment of the law. 1 John 4:16 says God is love, therefore His will (or law) is always motivated by love and is always for the benefit of people. Even in judgment, love is the motivation, and righteousness and justice are the results. So it is up to us to hear from the Lord, then to speak and to act according to His will. This is the process of legislating the will or the law of God on the Earth. This is how the *ekklesia* is to operate.

> *The heavens are the heavens of the Lord, but the Earth He has given to the sons of men.*
>
> Psalm 115:16

The Judicial Branch

Working in harmony with the legislative branch, the main purpose of the judicial branch is to release the judgments of God. This can take the form of decrees over families, congregations, cities, states, regions and nations. As part of the judicial branch, Moses sat to judge civil cases between individuals. When the load became too great, he chose men to help. In the New Testament, we see Paul fulfilling the function of the judicial branch—disciplining a congregation in 1 Corinthians 6.

Judging and judgments are referenced throughout the Bible, not just regarding people unwilling to repent, but toward the domain of darkness, evil spirits, and spiritual forces in heavenly places (Ephesians 6:12).

Finally, we see judgment as a prophetic act, such as when Joshua marched the children of Israel around the walls of Jericho and then blew the shofar. The walls tumbled down under the judgment of God.

However, there is a pervasive misunderstanding in the Body of Christ today concerning judgment, as evidenced by the many times we are taught never to judge. Indeed, the blanket avoidance of judgment has actually perverted our outlook and stunted our discernment, growing into an inferiority complex where people preface every observation they make with "I'm not judging, but..."

Certainly, judgment is a touchy subject, but it doesn't need to be. While nobody likes to be judged, the simple fact is that we do it every day, all day long. We make necessary judgments about what to wear, what to eat, what we put in our coffee in the morning, about people, the weather, what is true and what is not. You name it, we judge it. Judging is part of our nature, and it should be no surprise that it is also part of God's nature. He is the Great Judge, and there will be a Day of Judgment at the end of this age. The Bible refers to a courtroom setting with God as Judge, Jesus as a lawyer-advocate, and all mankind standing before Him for judgment (Revelation 20:11-15, 1 John 2:1). If that is not enough, we also have an entire book of the Bible called "Judges," and no, these people are not going to hell because they judged. God placed judges over Israel for His justice to be released and righteousness to prevail.

The problem is that we equate judgment with wrath and punishment, but this is not a fair association. While judgment often has a negative context, it can also be a positive experience. When a judge makes a judgment in the courtroom, it is negative for one party but positive for the other. You see, judging is not the problem; judging with evil motives is the problem. Jesus never condemned judgment; He only condemned hypocritical judgment (Matthew 7:1-5). While we are told not to judge unbelievers, the Bible makes it very clear that we are to judge believers.

For what have I to do with judging outsiders? Do you not judge those who are within the church?

But those who are outside, God judges. Remove the wicked man from among yourselves.

1 Corinthians 5:12-13

Does any one of you, when he has a case against his neighbor, dare to go to law before the unrighteous and not before the saints? Or do you not know that the saints will judge the world? If the world is judged by you, are you not competent to constitute the smallest law courts? Do you not know that we will judge angels? How much more matters of this life? So if you have law courts dealing with matters of this life, do you appoint them as judges who are of no account in the church? I say this to your shame. Is it so, that there is not among you one wise man who will be able to decide between his brethren, but brother goes to law with brother, and that before unbelievers?

1 Corinthians 6:1-6

In light of these and other scriptures, we cannot deny that judging is biblical—an essential part of our identity and purpose as the *ekklesia*. There are cases that need and should be resolved within the *ekklesia*. Further, there are times when we need to be involved in the world's justice system, as there are many cases that cannot be handled within the *ekklesia* at this time. This is why we are to pray for the earthly rulers over us.

In Matthew 18, Jesus refers to the *ekklesia* judging a legal matter.

"If your brother sins, go and show him his fault in private; if he listens to you, you have won your

brother. But if he does not listen to you, take one or two more with you, so that by the mouth of two or three witnesses every fact may be confirmed. If he refuses to listen to them, tell it to the church [ekklesia]; and if he refuses to listen even to the church [ekklesia], let him be to you as a Gentile and a tax collector. Truly I say to you, whatever you bind on earth shall have been bound in heaven; and whatever you loose on earth shall have been loosed in heaven. Again I say to you, that if two of you agree on earth about anything that they may ask, it shall be done for them by My Father who is in heaven. For where two or three have gathered together in My name, I am there in their midst."

Matthew 18:15-20

Here, Jesus gives the *ekklesia* a process for dealing with a brother (or sister) in sin. We see a brother who has sinned, and we are told the role the *ekklesia* is to play in his restoration. Jesus gives general directions for dealing with sin in the assembly, and explains when a judgment must be made. If it were true that we are not to judge, then we could not obey this teaching from the Lord Himself.. Even to confront our sinful brother, it is necessary that we make a judgment.

Of course, judging should always be done in a spirit of gentleness with humility for the purpose of redemption and restoration, never for revenge, anger, or self-righteousness. To judge righteously, the *ekklesia* must possess a Christ-like character. Love is the law of the Kingdom of God and should always be our motivation for all that we do, especially when it comes to judging. James 2:13 says that mercy triumphs over judgment. However, when there is no response to mercy, judgment must be made. Judgment is essential to the proper function of the *ekklesia*.

Notice the third step in the process Jesus outlines. If the person has not repented, we are to *"tell it to the ekklesia."* He did not say to tell it to everyone we know. Not every situation needs to be broadcast to the entire congregation. There are certain situations that need to be handled privately within a council of mature leaders. Certainly, if it is a sinful situation that affects the entire congregation, it needs to be addressed to the entire congregation. But if not, then it should be handled in private. Generally, sin should be handled within the realm in which it was committed. Sin is not the problem; sin is a symptom of a deeper problem—a heart condition. This is a serious issue that frankly, in our erroneous avoidance of judgment, we take too lightly.

Certainly, some issues need to be made public. One example is the ongoing, open sin of a leader such as an elder. It also may be necessary that the sin of an apostle, prophet, evangelist, or pastor that could affect a city, region, or even a nation be addressed to all.

> *Do not receive an accusation against an elder except on the basis of two or three witnesses. Those who continue in sin, rebuke in the presence of all, so that the rest also will be fearful of sinning.*
>
> 1 Timothy 5:19-20

This passage says specifically to *rebuke in the presence of all.* (Not a lot of wiggle room in that one.)

Following Jesus' instruction, if the person in sin will not repent after meeting with the *ekklesia,* he should be treated as a Gentile (an outsider) or a tax collector. (No offense meant to my brothers and sisters who work for the I.R.S.) In the cultural context, Jesus meant that he should be removed from the congregation with prejudice.

So...how often do we actually see this in our congregations today? I humbly submit that we rarely follow this God-given pattern. Why? Because it is difficult, and there is a general misunderstanding of church and judgment. The first time I had to do this in my congregation, it broke my heart. When I pleaded with my friend who was in sin to repent, he looked me in the eye and said, "No." I felt like my best friend just died when I had to remove him from our congregation. It is not easy, but must be done for the health and benefit of the entire congregation as well as for the one who is in sin.

In the passage from Matthew above, verse 18, notice that Jesus uses the binding and loosing terminology again as He did in Matthew 16. Binding and loosing, as we discussed earlier, are legal terms pertaining to binding a contract or being loosed from a contract. When the *ekklesia* comes together—where two or more agree—and hears from the Lord, if they make a judgment on what to do with this particular brother, it becomes legally binding both in Heaven and on Earth. It is that serious.

Taken out of context, however, this teaching can become a tool of the flesh. It has been common practice in some churches to use Jesus' statements in a way that is unbiblical. Take for instance verse 19 where Jesus says *"if two of you agree on Earth about anything that they may ask, it shall be done for them by My Father who is in heaven."* Let's be clear. We do not get whatever we ask for just because we get one or two others to agree with us in prayer. Jesus did not give us a blank check, as much as we would like to believe this at times (even when our motives seem pure, like if we need a new motorcycle or something for "ministry" purposes).

The Apostle John wrote to correct this error.

This is the confidence which we have before Him, that, if we ask anything according to His will, He hears us. And if we know that He hears us in whatever we ask, we know that we have the requests which we have asked from Him.

1 John 5:14-15

We receive from God when we pray according to His will, not our own will or desire. Of course we can always ask God for anything. However, He is not obligated to give it simply because we have someone else who agrees with us.

The word "anything" in Matthew 18 is actually two Greek words; *pas* and *pragma*. Both of these words used together mean "any judicial matter." Contrast this to the common mistranslation "anything we ask for." When used in context, Jesus is saying that when two or three come together to look into this judicial matter about what to do with the brother in sin, He will be there and give His judgment.

If you have two children and they both commit the same sin, you may have to deal with them differently based on their age, maturity level and personality. What might be the best course of discipline or restoration for one child may not be best for another. It is the same way in the *ekklesia*. Every person is different. Every case is unique because people are unique. Yes, each case needs to be addressed, but it needs to be handled differently based on the unique circumstances. Ultimately, the Lord knows the best for each individual and what will help them towards the purpose of redemption. It is the job of the *ekklesia* to be sensitive and obedient to the Lord to discern His will and apply it.

We see this principle illustrated in the ministry of the Apostle Paul. One time, he rebuked the Corinthians for not judging a fellow believer who was committing open sin. Yet another time, he told them the brother had suffered enough and that they should receive him back. Both times; however, judgments were made. It is important that we do not develop a generic approach in these matters. In my ministry, I have had the Lord tell me not to say anything to an individual, and at other times He has said to address an issue immediately. In order to be effective, the *ekklesia* must be led by the Holy Spirit.

As humans, we like patterns and processes, using them over and over. This is a reason why so many self-help books—3 steps to this and 7 steps to that—are so popular. Just tell me the formula so I can do it and have success. Yet if all we needed was a formula, we wouldn't need the Holy Spirit. Too often we interpret the Bible with the same cookie cutter approach. While the Bible gives us principles of truth, they are to be applied with the direction of the Holy Spirit. We are in relationship with a living being, not a prescribed set of instructions.

His Presence

Another common misunderstanding of Jesus' teaching comes from Matthew 18:20:

> *"For where two or three have gathered together in My name, I am there in their midst."*
>
> Matthew 18:20

Taken out of context, we can get the impression that we can only experience the presence of Jesus in groups. Yet this understanding is in conflict with other scriptures on the subject. We do not need to get one or two others to join us to have the presence of Jesus. We can have His presence when we are alone. For example:

> *Christ in us the hope of glory...*
>
> Colossians 1:27

*Do you not know that you are a temple of God and
that the Spirit of God dwells in you?*

1 Corinthians 3:16

The truth is that the presence of Jesus dwells with all those who are born again—on an individual basis as well as corporately. Certainly, His manifest presence is unique for different times and places. However, just because two or three are gathered together doesn't mean Jesus is present, even if they are Christians. They could be gathered in the wrong spirit, for the wrong motives, or casual endeavors or projects. While God cherishes our intentions, He is also in the business of maturing us.

To sum up what Jesus is telling us from this passage, when we have a brother that is in sin, there is a process for restoration. If he will not repent, then at least two or three elders from the *ekklesia* are to gather to seek the Lord for specific direction on exactly how to deal with this individual. When they do this, Jesus promises He will be in their midst to give His direction and righteous judgment. When the two or three receive the direction from the Lord and there is agreement, then they should implement the judgment. At that point, it becomes legally binding in the eyes of the Lord.

The Court System

In Matthew 5:21-22—The Sermon on the Mount—Jesus gives us a type of constitution for the Kingdom of Heaven on Earth by outlining what life is like in the Kingdom on Earth. He speaks of two courts, and in doing so, He explains that a court system still exists in the Kingdom of Heaven.

*"You have heard that the ancients were told, 'You
shall not commit murder and whoever commits
murder shall be liable to the court.' But I say to you*

that everyone who is angry with his brother shall be guilty before the court; and whoever says to his brother, 'You good-for-nothing,' shall be guilty before the supreme court; and whoever says, 'You fool,' shall be guilty enough to go into the fiery hell."

Matthew 5:21-22

The Jewish court in Jesus' day was the Sanhedrin—a body of Jewish leaders similar to a local district court that we have today in our U.S. cities. The highest court in Jewish culture was the Great Sanhedrin, which is similar to the United States Supreme Court. This court system was the method the nation of Israel used to accomplish God's justice. Every Hebrew town had a Sanhedrin; the Great Sanhedrin was located in Jerusalem.

The word Sanhedrin means "a sitting together," as in a council. As you can see, this is what Jesus said to convene when a brother is in sin and will not repent. The elders (two or three) should convene knowing that Jesus was present, in order to receive His counsel and then render judgment.

Just as it was then, judging is a necessary part of the *ekklesia* and kingdom life today. It does not need to be a negative task. In fact, judgment isn't always concerning people. There are times when the Lord will cause us to release judgments over wickedness in general, as well as over cities and nations. There have been times when our government has passed unrighteous laws, and in prayer, I heard the Lord tell me to command that law to die. This is similar to the way some Old Testament prophets did things.

As the *ekklesia*, we do not have to take every bit of evil that is thrown our way. Indeed, we cannot. We need to hear from God concerning laws and decisions that are made by people in authority and take a stand by implementing righteousness. If the *ekklesia* does not rule, someone else will. The Lord never told us to put our trust and hope in politicians but in Him and Him alone!

Chapter 10

Where Do We Begin?

We now know that Jesus never intended to build the church in the conventional sense. Instead, His intentions were greater; He boldly proclaimed to His disciples that He would build His *ekklesia*, and by that, He meant a systematic, world-reaching government of Heaven that would release a kingdom culture of righteousness and justice.

Unfortunately, we have lost sight of Jesus' original aims. Our Bible translation was corrupted by the mistranslation of a single word—church—representing an intentional power grab by hell intent on controlling the Christian religious structure as the serpent did in the Garden: by deception.

Many in the church today have become so fed up with the overly structured, heavily controlled and overall powerless church that they have just left it altogether. There is a ditch on either side of the path of life—legalism on one side and rampant liberality on the other. Today as we gradually move away from the confines of structured religion and despotic worldly leadership, we still confront impediments to Jesus' ultimate plan. We misunderstand the nature of the *ekklesia,* and we bring to our Christian worldview a host of erroneous teachings which may comfort us in the immediate sense, but hold us back from reaching the full potential intended by God.

Make no mistake, however. Just as man's original commission to go forth and subdue the Earth is irrevocable, so are the plans and purposes of Jesus regarding His *ekklesia*. He will accomplish that for which He gave His life. The question is are we willing to be a part of this revolution as the Spirit of God sweeps across our Earth declaring what has been known from the beginning: that the gifts and callings of God are without repentance, and His kingdom is an everlasting kingdom.

Mindset

The key to functioning as the *ekklesia* is to change our mindset. As Paul told us in Romans:

> *Do not be conformed to the world but be transformed by the renewing of our minds so that we may prove what the will of God is, that which is good and acceptable and perfect.*
>
> Romans 12:2

First, we must change our thinking from that of a slave to a son of the King. Slaves do not inherit, nor do they subdue and rule. Next, we have to revise our image of Christ's body from a church to the *ekklesia*; from pastoral to apostolic; from Christian to Kingdom. Finally, we must transform our worldview according to the Word of God, and not allow it to be conformed strictly by our experiences, preferences, culture, or religious denominations.

Of course, this can be a difficult task. Our false mindsets are deeply engrained. It will take time and effort, but it will be worth it. When our thinking changes, our behavior will follow.

We must make it our priority to *seek first the Kingdom of God and His righteousness* (Matthew 6:33). These are Jesus' words, not mine. In this simple phrase, Jesus is setting the priority for every believer. Seeking the Kingdom includes seeking the King of the Kingdom. Out of relationship with the Lord, we learn to abide in Him, and the abundant life promised us begins to saturate our lives. As we learned earlier, our authority on Earth flows from the abiding presence of the Lord and our submission to His authority. In fulfilling the great commission, the first area we must subdue and rule is our own lives, establishing the Kingdom for the King on an individual basis.

As we align our priorities according to Jesus' mandate, the Holy Spirit will give us revelation on the *ekklesia* and the Kingdom of Heaven. We are His passion, and as we grow to match His dedication, everything we think will be in harmony with the King, so our every action will reflect Kingdom living.

Moving Experience

Many Christians will move across the country for a better job, a more prestigious school, lighter taxes, or more pleasant weather. Yet we give little thought to how our actions might affect the Kingdom of God. We figure we'll just find a suitable church when we arrive. The problem with this thinking is that God is strategic. He places us where we are to be—if we let Him.

In light of this revelation, we may need to rethink our priorities away from careers, profits, and preferences, to Kingdom purposes. Are we seeking our own gain from our lives, or are we truly seeking to reflect the culture of the Kingdom? The Lord needs us to be where He calls us, doing what He has called us to do. That is how we will be most effective and feel the most fulfilled. We can have the best jobs, the greatest opportunities, attend the top schools and inhabit thriving communities, but unless we are aligned with His purpose for our lives, we will not produce lasting fruit, if any at all. While there is nothing wrong with the things that healthy people naturally seek, our call is to reach the people around us, showing them God by the way we live our lives, and establishing a Kingdom culture everywhere we go. The heart-cry of our generation echoes the words of Philip in John 14:8, *"show us the Father and it is good enough for us!"* Jesus answered him saying,

> *"Have I been so long with you, and yet you have not come to know Me, Philip? He who has seen Me has seen the Father; how can you say, 'Show us the Father'?"*
>
> John 14:9

Our neighborhoods are not just places to live; they are our mission fields for establishing the Kingdom. As we are obedient, the Lord will give us a strategy for transforming our schools, our businesses, even our clubs and sports teams for Kingdom purposes and the Father's glory...if we seek Him and allow our mindsets to change and come into conformity with His.

In the Sermon on the Mount, Jesus gave us the cultural values and lifestyle of the Kingdom of Heaven on Earth. He taught us how to live out holiness in a practical way. As we follow His teaching, allowing His life to flow through us, we establish Kingdom values in our homes, neighborhoods, workplaces, cities and nations, although it won't always be easy. In the book of Acts, immediately following Pentecost, the lifestyle of the people of God caused dramatic changes in their environment, igniting a cultural awakening and riot.

> *They began dragging Jason and some brethren before the city authorities, shouting, "These men who have upset the world have come here also; and*

Jason has welcomed them, and they all act contrary to the decrees of Caesar, saying that there is another king, Jesus.

Acts 17:6-7

Your Kingdom Come

The purpose of the *ekklesia* is not to make everything Christian, or even to provide an alternative religion, but to gradually transform society to look more like the Kingdom of Heaven. Remember God's original commission to us: to subdue and rule (Genesis 1:28). To adequately address the realities of human existence, our thinking must radically shift away from the classic polarization of *Christian* verses *secular*. These definitions mean little; in fact, they alienate more people than they reach, sending a message of "*us* versus them." To be effective as the *ekklesia*, we must adapt a wider, more inclusive approach to our fellow man—all under the authority and rule of God's kingdom.

What do the terms *Christian* and *secular* mean anyway? For example, how do we decide if music, movies, books, or art is Christian or not? Typically, we call something secular if Christian values are not portrayed, or when a non-Christian is the artist, even if their song is a beautiful representation of Christian values. But because the person is not a Christian, we condemn it with the sad label *secular*. This is unfortunate.

Christianity's past method of waging war against evil by wielding the vague term *secular* at everything threatening is not working. We have allowed the values of a counterfeit kingdom—the domain of darkness—to spread throughout our society while we retreat to our private Christian existence, secure in our false sense of conformity.

Jesus said *"Thy Kingdom come, Thy will be done on Earth as it is in Heaven."* He did not say to make the world necessarily Christian but establish a Kingdom of Heaven culture, teaching the nations to be godly. There is one Kingdom of God and one will of God.

> *The leaves of the tree of life are for the healing of the nations.*
>
> Revelation 22:2

Certainly, I am not advocating abandoning Christian values or the Great Commission. Rather, I am recommending that everything in our culture be reformed so that it may come under the influence of God's Kingdom. When properly executed, the *ekklesia* will allow the Kingdom of Heaven on Earth to invade all of society, influencing our culture to reflect the values of the Kingdom in music, television, movies, books, video games, schools, sports, government, business, the arts, and education.

> *Seek the welfare of the city where I have sent you into exile, and pray to the Lord on its behalf; for in its welfare you will have welfare.*
>
> Jeremiah 29:7

The Kingdom of God was designed to be lived out in a practical way. It is not something we attend on Sunday morning. It is so much greater. We have a mandate to influence the Seven Mountains of Society:

- *Religion*
- *Family*
- *Education*
- *Government*
- *Business*

- *Arts and Entertainment*
- *Media*

The *ekklesia* is called to transform these key components of society to become more like the Kingdom of Heaven. And yet, Christians are not the only ones engaged in this transformation. Radical Muslims today are actively changing world cultures for the sake of Islam. Historically and currently they have and are accomplishing this by force. In contrast, the Kingdom of Heaven will advance through the power of the Holy Spirit, employing love, compassion, mercy and justice. The *ekklesia* is not about forcing a law on people; it is about employing the love of God to bring freedom, healing and restoration to the world.

Of course, this all starts at home. If we are not transformed, can we effectively transform the world? If lying, cheating, stealing, manipulating, coveting, and illicit sexual behavior is not acceptable in Heaven, why do we, as the people of God, permit it in our own lives now? As citizens of the Kingdom of Heaven, it is amazing how many things we tolerate and participate in, knowing they are not permitted in Heaven.

Didn't Jesus say that we are to go into all the world making disciples of nations, teaching them to obey all that He commanded? Rather than waiting to leave this Earth and enter Heaven, we are to bring Heaven to Earth! Let's remember the words of Jesus: *the meek shall inherit the Earth,* (Matthew 5:5). He did not say the meek shall inherit Heaven. In other words, we should be living "heavenly," holy lives here on Earth, now.

We can do this! The *ekklesia* is divinely equipped to carry out all that God has commissioned. We can change our culture to be more like the Kingdom of Heaven. Certainly, it will not be a utopia until Jesus returns, but it can reflect the values of the Kingdom in greater and greater measure. We do not have to settle for anything less. If we want our culture to change, we must change first. Our personal lives must begin to reflect Kingdom values. Transformed people transform society. We must operate in a different spirit than what is operating in our city.

> He who is slow to anger is better than the mighty, and he who rules his spirit, than he who captures a city.
>
> Proverbs 16:32

Let us begin in the house of God. What if entire congregations everywhere began to think like God and act like God? What if our congregations began to look more like the Kingdom of Heaven than the world? Let's see what that would be like.

Alignment

If you have ever had your back go out of alignment as I have, you know how painful it can be. Your whole body is in agony. When the spine is misaligned, your body doesn't function as created, and other body parts have to take up the slack (not to mention your longsuffering spouse). It is the same way in the Body of Christ. When individuals are out of alignment, the whole Body suffers and doesn't function as God intended.

In my opinion, this is why so many Christians feel so unfulfilled in their lives. Many have been taught to chase their dreams and do what they are passionate about. Until we die to self and submit to the dreams and passions of God, we will not experience the fulfillment that comes with the abundant life He created us for. God created us for His good pleasure and for His purpose. When we are not fulfilling our divine purpose, we have a sense of a lack of fulfillment.

I was passionate about working on motorcycles and owning my own business and had no desire to be in youth ministry until I submitted to the will of God for my life. Then I became passionate about youth ministry. The same thing happened to me when I knew the Lord was leading me to leave youth ministry and plant a church. I had no desire for that whatsoever. I was more passionate at that time about foreign missions. I had been on many mission trips and led most of them. I even tried to pursue full-time work in missions. But the Lord said *no,* and He directed me to do what I was not passionate about. Once I said *yes* and stepped in that direction, then I became passionate about it.

We must fully surrender to the will of God for our lives to discover what He created us to do and to experience the true passion of God. I believe we often misplace our passions, and focus instead on the work or the ministry when our main focus and passion ought to be on God Himself. Only then, we are free to go where He leads us and do what He tells us. In the end, it is not about where we are and what we're doing, it is about pleasing the One who gave His life for us because we love Him. Jesus didn't want to go to the cross, and He prayed to Father for another way. Father did not answer Him because there *was* no other way. So, Jesus said, *Not my will by yours be done.* His focus wasn't on the cross; it was on Father. Like a master chiropractor, God is calling His people back into alignment: personally, congregationally, regionally and globally. As we align and respond to His call, the *ekklesia* will begin to function more effectively.

As we have discussed, all authority is delegated authority. It is not our own; it originates from Jesus and flows to us as we position ourselves with Him. We transition towards proper alignment when we pursue our position as sons of God. This is where all authority begins. Then as sons, through our bloodline relationship with the Lord, we go where He tells us to go; we live where He tells us to live.

And finally, we come to understand our spiritual occupation; that which He has called us to do. These three primary areas: position, location and occupation, must align for us to have the maximum effectiveness that God intended. Our authority and relationships are dependent on this critical agreement. Let's take a closer look at each.

Position

In the beginning (Genesis 1:26-28) God created man in positional alignment with the Holy Trinity. He blessed man and gave him the ability to be fruitful and multiply. He also gave him delegated authority to subdue the Earth, allowing him to rule over the fish, the birds, and land animals.

Our God-given authority flows from our relationship with the Lord as His sons. Jesus said we must abide in the Vine, for apart from Him we can do nothing (John 15). Our position, then, begins when we are born again and submit to the Lordship of Jesus Christ. It is then that we begin to discover our specific calling in the Body of Christ and to function in it. If we are called to music, business, homemaking, or politics—even motorcycle mechanics—we need to begin seeking God to see how He wants us to prepare for and accomplish what He has called us to do. Sometimes there is a long gap, education, training, preparation, etc. between when we hear God call us to a work and when we finally get to "do" the thing. If we try to "get busy" too quickly, we fall into problems, like Moses. It doesn't mean that it will be easy and there are no shortcuts, but it will be rewarding. In the process, we will discover that we do not have to be concerned with stopping what we are not supposed to be involved in because we are too busy doing what we are called to do.

Location

In Genesis 2:15, God gave man some prime real estate with a great location: the Garden of Eden. The geographical confines of Adam's assignment were crucial. Even though God said man would rule and reign over all the Earth, He first put man in a relatively small place—the Garden of Eden. Adam's authority to rule was limited to the Garden at first.

Similarly, our authority is regional and affects our particular calling. Therefore, it is vital that we live in the region to which God has called us. I realize this is a radical idea. Today, many Christians move across the country for a job or career, but give little thought to Kingdom purposes. In truth, our God-ordained location is critical to our sense of fulfillment and a "job well done," and includes His specific details for the country, state, city and region that we inhabit, ensuring that we fully align with the people and culture around us.

Sometimes, we are functioning in our calling but doing so in the wrong location. In that case, we would still be out of alignment. We are given authority within our calling only in the location God has ordained for us. For example, because God has called me to Independence, Missouri, I have authority in that city. But if I go to another city that God has not called me to, I would not have authority there in my calling unless it was given to me by the One who led me.

Occupation

In Genesis 2:15, God gave man a job; he was to cultivate and keep the garden. And while he may have been great at mulching and pruning, he didn't fulfill the "keep" aspect of his job description very well. Years ago as I was reading this portion of scripture the Lord spoke to me and said: *I want you to cultivate a relationship with Me and keep it.* You see, the life of Christ flows through "keeping" or maintaining a healthy relationship with God. Out of this relationship flows submission to His will for our lives.

In Christianity today, we typically view our jobs and careers as secular employment unless we are in full-time ministry—a term I use loosely, as it carries unfortunate implications. Actually, all of us are in full-time ministry, whether we stay home and raise children, hang sheetrock, devise exit strategies for failed corporate mergers, or stand in front of people and teach the word of God. Instead of separating the segments of our lives and labeling some as "ministry" and others as "occupations," we need to adjust our thinking to see ourselves as called by God to whatever occupation, or job we hold in order to influence that particular area with a Kingdom culture and reach people. Regardless of who cuts our check, God is actually paying us to be in the ministry right where we work. Fulfilling our occupation includes our calling in the Body of Christ and functioning in our spiritual gifts and talents that the Lord has given us.

Man's disobedience caused him to lose his correct alignment with God. By one decision man tragically lost his position, his location and his occupation (Genesis 3). Through repentance and the forgiveness offered through the sacrifice of Christ, we regain all three enabling us to prosper and live the promised abundant life like the prodigal son of Luke 15.

Authority

Authority is obviously a very important aspect of the *ekklesia*. As I already mentioned, Jesus said that all authority in Heaven and on Earth had been given to Him. The root word of authority is *author*. Jesus is the author of authority. All authority in the Kingdom of Heaven is delegated by Jesus and functions as we submit to Him; and we are given authority in proportion to our specific calling and field of ministry. So it is important that we know the field that we are called to.

All authority in the Kingdom begins with humility and servanthood.

And He [Jesus] said to them, "The kings of the Gentiles lord it over them; and those who have authority over them are called 'Benefactors.' But it is not this way with you, but the one who is the greatest among you must become like the youngest, and the leader like the servant."

Luke 22:25-26

Character development is crucial to holding and exercising authority. Someone once told me that to be a person of authority; I must be a person *under* authority. That has stuck with me to this day. When I was in the military, I learned a lot about authority. In fact, I thought I was joining the military for one reason, and I discovered later that God had other reasons: one was to teach me about authority. (OK, so I was a bit rebellious back then.) I learned many tough lessons, but the most useful was how to serve and obey those in authority over me—even when I didn't like them or agree with them.

In Matthew 8:5-13, Jesus' conversation with a high-level Roman soldier—a centurion with 100 men under his command—tells us much about how respect for and understanding of authority and how it operates in the Kingdom of God.

And when Jesus entered Capernaum, a centurion came to Him, imploring Him, and saying, "Lord, my servant is lying paralyzed at home, fearfully tormented." Jesus said to him, "I will come and heal him." But the centurion said, "Lord, I am not worthy for You to come under my roof, but just say the word, and my servant will be healed. For I also am a man under authority, with soldiers under me; and I say to this one, 'Go!' and he goes, and to another, 'Come!'

and he comes, and to my slave, 'Do this!' and he does it." Now when Jesus heard this, He marveled and said to those who were following, "Truly I say to you, I have not found such great faith with anyone in Israel."

Matthew 8:5-11

This Centurion understood authority and its function. Notice that he identified himself as a man under authority as well as one who had authority over other soldiers. He understood where he was in the chain of command and how authority flowed. This centurion was in the Roman military under the command of the Emperor of Rome. Therefore, when he gave a command, he spoke with the authority of the Emperor. A soldier who disobeyed the centurion would be disobeying the Emperor and Rome itself, not just the centurion. Likewise, when he received an order, he also understood that it was supported by Rome.

As a person under authority, the centurion also recognized those who had real authority. He saw that Jesus had great authority and realized that He must be under the authority of God because when Jesus spoke, it was backed by God; demons, weather, sickness, and disease all obeyed Him. Further, the centurion's understanding of authority enabled him to trust Jesus completely. He understood that if Jesus merely spoke, His word would be backed by God, and his servant would be healed. He understood that Jesus didn't need to be physically present.

What remarkable faith, all stemming from an understanding of authority! When Jesus heard the centurion express such confidence, He marveled, saying He had not found anyone with such great faith in all of Israel. Like the centurion we also must have a full understanding and respect for authority in order to cooperate in God's Kingdom work and to engage in life-changing, faith-filled actions. This is the faith and authority that we *can* function in as the *ekklesia* seeing the will of God accomplished in our cities, nations and world.

However, to walk in such faith, we must operate in a different spirit than the world's system. Further, we cannot combat a religious spirit if we are functioning in a religious spirit. We cannot overcome lawlessness in our society if we are lawless. Our first change must be within.

The world walks in the pride of the flesh. Yet for Christians, humility is the beginning of great authority in the Kingdom of Heaven. Pride causes lawlessness and rebellion. We cannot live like the world and expect demons to flee.

Submission and Obedience

> *If you consent and obey, you will eat the best of the land;*
>
> Isaiah 1:19

There is a key difference between submission and obedience. Submission refers to surrendering our will to the Lord's will. It is our willingness to obey, arising from a heart condition and attitude that puts His desires above our own. Obedience, on the other hand, refers to our actions. It is the act of doing what another tells us to do. Following instructions, rules and laws are examples of obedience. But notice the subtle difference between the two. We can be obedient to the Lord but not submitted to Him. But we cannot be submitted to Him without being obedient.

The Lord is concerned with the condition of our hearts, not just our actions and behaviors conforming to an instruction set like a robot. God's Spirit always gets to the heart of the matter. If He has our heart, our obedience will follow because we love Him and are motivated by that love. And further, when we give our hearts to the Lord—submitted and obedient to Him—we are then free and able to submit to man.

> *They first gave themselves to the Lord and to us by the will of God.*

> 2 Corinthians 8:5

In the scripture above, the apostle Paul spoke about the Thessalonians who gave finances out of their poverty; so much so that it surprised him. He said that they were able to submit to the apostles because they first submitted to the Lord. This is a key point. Many are not submitted to the Lord, therefore they cannot submit to man. And in their present mindset, they don't believe they should.

As God's ambassadors, we do what He wants done. The Lord doesn't give His full authority to rebellious or unfaithful people. The more the Lord trusts us, the greater the authority we can walk in, and the greater works we will do. Growing through submission into obedience is the key to acquiring Christ's likeness and authority in the *ekklesia*.

Implementation

I used to own a commercial building in Kansas City, Missouri that had two apartments on the second floor. Several times over the years, I had to evict my tenants for not paying rent. We would go to court, and I would win the case every time. When the judge rendered his verdict, he would tell my tenant to pay what he owed me or move out by a certain date. However, I discovered that these were mere words. There was nothing in place that actually implemented the judgment. If the tenant didn't pay or move out, I had to go back to court and start another legal process for eviction.

I learned the hard way that implementing the legislation or judgment is critical to possessing the land that God gives us.

> I will send hornets ahead of you so that they will drive out the Hivites, the Canaanites, and the Hittites before you. "I will not drive them out before you in a single year, that the land may not become desolate and the beasts of the field become too numerous for you. "I will drive them out before you little by little, until you become fruitful and take possession of the land.
>
> Exodus 23:28-30

When we review the history of the Jews, we see that God never gave the Children of Israel victories that they were unable to hold. God doesn't want us to simply win. He wants us to possess the prize after our victories. Notice from the passage above that if Israel were to wipe out their enemies too quickly, another enemy would appear. We must be ready to implement what we legislate, or we might replace one enemy for another, and the last state might just be as bad or worse than the first

Here is another scripture to illustrate legislation and implementation.

> "Now when the unclean spirit goes out of a man, it passes through waterless places seeking rest, and does not find it. Then it says, 'I will return to my house from which I came'; and when it comes, it finds it unoccupied, swept, and put in order. Then it goes and takes along with it seven other spirits more wicked than itself, and they go in and live there; and the last state of that man becomes worse than the first. That is the way it will also be

with this evil generation.

Matthew 12:43-45

We see here what can happen when an evil spirit is cast out of a person. (Recall our earlier discussion of binding and loosing). In this case, a legally binding judgment has been made in the spiritual realm. The person has been loosed (freed) from a demon. However, if the Holy Spirit is not invited to occupy the place, the cast-out demon will return along with other evil spirits more wicked than himself.

You see, we can prophesy and legislate the will of God in our cities, and they can become free from criminal activity and all other evil, but if we are not leading people to Christ with life changing transformation, what have we gained? If we are not implementing righteousness and justice in the seven mountains of society, we will find things in a worse condition than when we first began.

> *Righteousness and justice are the foundation of His throne.*

Psalm 97:2

As the *ekklesia*, we need to train and prepare people to go into the Seven Mountains of society to function in apostolic authority in order to see society reformed according to the Kingdom of God. The Seven Mountains of Society are the "gates" to our culture, and we have authority over them. We know that Jesus promised that the gates of hell could not prevail against His *ekklesia*. What we allow to come through them influences everything. As the *ekklesia* following the will of God, we can determine what society will be like.

And to Him was given dominion, glory and a kingdom, that all the peoples, nations and men of every language might serve Him. His dominion is an everlasting dominion which will not pass away; and His kingdom is one which will not be destroyed.

Daniel 7:14

Unity

The Tower of Babel taught us the awesome power of unity. Sure, it was an evil power, but it still points to the power God gave man. Unity is a principle that works whether we are children of God or not. When people get together in agreement, whether by design or under extraordinary circumstances, they can accomplish incredible things.

Jesus prayed that the *ekklesia* would be unified, possessing the same bond that He and His Father had! That is powerful!

I do not ask on behalf of these alone, but for those also who believe in Me through their word; that they may all be one; even as You, Father, are in Me and I in You, that they also may be in Us, so that the world may believe that You sent Me.

John 17:20-21

Note that He did not pray for uniformity where we all look, talk and dress alike. Creation shows us that God loves variety. And if you don't think He has a sense of humor, you haven't paid too much attention to the animal kingdom. The unity Jesus prayed for was oneness amidst our many differences; one body, many body parts. Consider the Trinity—even the Father, Son and Holy Spirit are not the same person, yet they are so unified in thought, action and purpose that they function as one. This is the way the Body of

Christ is to function—as one Body. Unity is a product of love and must have love as its foundation.

> *Beyond all these things put on love, which is the perfect bond of unity.*
>
> Colossians 3:14

True love requires humility. It takes Christ-like love and humility to walk in agreement with one another even though we have differences. Satan has been wickedly successful at creating a counterfeit kingdom based on pride and territorialism. This is why we are warned against this in two places in the New Testament.

> *God is opposed to the proud, but gives grace to the humble.*
>
> 1 Peter 5:5, James 4:6

Whether we call ourselves Baptist, Methodist, Charismatic, or Catholic; tall or short; republican or democrat; black, brown, red or white; we must stop allowing our differences to be an excuse for disunity. We must find common ground in the core truths of the Kingdom and stop arguing like immature children over peripheral doctrines. If we believe that Jesus is the Son of God—the way, the truth and the life, and that no one can come to the Father but through Him, we have a place to start. I am not preaching Universalism or Unitarianism. I do hold securely to truths stated plainly in the Word of God—those that we must not compromise; but beyond these, we can and should be able to achieve unity with those who do not think or look exactly like we do. And they might even teach us something.

Before I leave the subject of unity, let's look at the greatest issue dividing people after religious doctrine and racism: gender. Nothing can alienate human beings like the differences between men and women. I have more in common with a male of any race or culture than I do with a female. When God knocked Adam out, He took a lot more from him than a rib. He removed a vital part of his being.

Men and women are vastly different in many ways. And still, when they come together in marriage, God says that they become one. This kind of unity is a process not an event; it doesn't occur spontaneously or effortlessly. To be candid, there have been times when I thought He must have been joking. My wife and I do not agree on everything; we even have differences on some scripture interpretations. But after thirty years of marriage, we have learned to function together in unity and share a oneness of heart. Oneness in marriage is so important because it is an example of our relationship with the Lord and an expression of who He is.

Marriage also shows us some of the challenges we can expect to face as we attempt to have unity with others who are born again, but believe differently than we do. But also like marriage, all true unity with other believers will be founded on love. Look at John 17:20-21 again. Jesus said that our oneness with Him and with one another will cause the world to know that God the Father sent Him to the world and loves them! Wow! When it's all said and done, I think unity, like marriage, will be worth the effort.

This unity is the work of the Holy Spirit in these last days as the Third Great Awakening is upon us. Through unity, we will see the power of God manifest in the harvest of souls. We will usher in the reformation of society through the Seven Mountains, experiencing an outpouring of signs, wonders and miracles like the world has never seen.

> *Behold, how good and how pleasant it is for brothers*
> *to dwell together in unity! It is like the precious oil*

upon the head, coming down upon the beard, even Aaron's beard, coming down upon the edge of his robes. It is like the dew of Hermon coming down upon the mountains of Zion; for there the Lord commanded the blessing—life forever.

Psalm 133:1-3

Some Final Thoughts

I have a couple of concerns I want to mention.

First, we must be careful that we are not just replacing the word "church" for *ekklesia*. *Ekklesia* is neither a fad nor a fancy new Christian buzzword. My concern is that there will be those who learn a new word and start calling church gatherings the *ekklesia*, but continue doing the same things they have always done. Let's not place a new label on an old wineskin. There are things we do in church that are important and will not change. For instance: teaching, preaching, worshipping, and fellowship. We see some of these things listed in Acts 2:46. However, as we have discussed here, there is a fundamental difference between the functions of the *ekklesia* and the church. Whether we call it "church" or *ekklesia* is not important, it is how we function.

Another concern I have is that in our embrace of a fresh idea, we develop a model of what we think the *ekklesia* should look like and try to reproduce that in every city and nation—a cookie cutter formula. While there are Biblical principles and elements to *ekklesia*, I do believe it will be different among different cultures, from city to city, and even from congregation to congregation. Remember that even in the last chapter of Revelation, we see a reference to "the nations," implying a difference in cultural identity even on the restored Earth under Jesus' rule.

Finally, 2 Thessalonians 2-3 tells us that before Jesus returns, there will be an apostasy. An apostasy is a falling away, but more specifically, it is a political revolt. This refers to a time when many of the people of God will rebel against the rule and law of God. And to be clear, the Bible is referring to those who have been born again as children of God, not those who do not know God. The verse goes on to speak about the man of lawlessness who will be revealed before Jesus returns. Lawlessness means living a life contrary to God's prescribed order. Put simply, it means not living by the law of love. Love does no wrong, therefore love is the fulfillment of the law (Romans 13:10). Jesus also spoke about lawlessness in the last days in Matthew 24. He said the love of many would grow cold.

> *Then you will be handed over to be persecuted and put to death, and you will be hated by all nations because of me. At that time many will turn away from the faith and will betray and hate each other, and many false prophets will appear and deceive many people because of the increase of wickedness, the love of most will grow cold, but the one who stands firm to the end will be saved.*
>
> Matthew 24: 9-13

Something we can be sure of, however is that King Jesus is coming again, and His Kingdom will be the only kingdom on Earth. This is the direction of our age, and we—the *ekklesia*— have the privilege of partnering with Him to accomplish it.

> *Then the seventh angel sounded; and there were loud voices in heaven, saying, "The kingdom of the world has become the kingdom of our Lord and of His Christ; and He will reign forever and ever.*
>
> Revelation 11:15

> *He will reign over the house of Jacob forever, and His*
> *kingdom will have no end.*

Luke 1:33

There is much more to discover concerning ekklesia. May God richly bless you as you consider these things.

Contact Information

Joe Nicola
New Covenant Ministries
Independence, Missouri
(816) 836-8303
Email: joenicola@aol.com

Made in the USA
San Bernardino, CA
18 July 2016